Baseball's Hitting Secrets

Baseball's Hitting Secrets

How to Put a Round Baseball Bat on a Round Ball — Squarely

Ted Burda
"The Hit Doctor"

SPORTS RESOURCES books
are published by
Van der Plas Publications
San Francisco

Printed in U.S.A.

Published by
Van der Plas Publications
1282 7th Avenue
San Francisco, CA 94122, USA
E-mail: pubrel@vanderplas.net
Website: http://www.vanderplas.net

Distributed or represented to the book trade by:
USA: Seven Hills Book Distributing, Cincinnati, OH
UK: Chris Lloyd Sales and Marketing Services, Poole, Dorset
Canada: Hushion House Book Publishers, Toronto, ON
Australia: Tower Books, Frenchs Forest, NSW

Cover design: Kent Lytle

Photographs by Mary Alpert

Publisher's Cataloging-in-Publication Data
Burda, Ted. Baseball's Hitting Secrets: How to Put a Round Baseball Bat on a
Round Ball—Squarely.
Includes Bibliography and Index p. cm.
ISBN 1-892495-34-1
Library of Congress Control Number 2001-131628

To Linda, Tim, Brett, who light up my life the way
Mark McGwire lights up a fast ball

About the Author

Ted Burda has been a batting instructor in Southern California since the early 1990s. He has been immersed in coaching baseball and other youth sports with his boys' team since 1990. Before that, he had been the owner of a furniture company and an expert furniture builder.

His love affair with baseball started with his own little league experience as a lefty pitcher in, of all places, Brussels, Belgium, as a "military brat." His fifteen minutes of glory came when he pitched his team to a shut-out win in the championship game. Babe Ruth league in Texas and high school baseball in Virginia followed, and one year he made it to a California CIF High School sectional golf tournament.

As a young adult, he played some local tournament tennis and ran nastar ski slalom courses. He still enjoys playing golf, tennis, and skiing.

Since 1993, he has had the pleasure of instructing thousands of batters in the perplexing yet wondrous art and science of hitting a baseball. As part of his batting instruction, he enjoys developing and inventing original training aids and drills, such as those included in this book.

He lives in Orange County, California, with his wife of 30 years, Linda, and his two teenage sons, and he has enjoyed coaching for many all-star baseball teams with both his boys over several years.

Ted can be reached by E-mail at THEHITDOCTER@aol.com

Table of Contents

1.

Introduction

In this book, I share the inside secrets of my trade as a batting instructor. I'm in a unique position to know what really works and what doesn't. Hitting instructors enjoy a secret advantage. We constantly work with all kinds of hitters. One moment a league superstar, the next a six-year-old tee baller, standing there holding his bat cross handed.

Nothing earth-shattering there, right? Don't be so sure. By having so much experience with so many types of hitters, you start to become aware of the differences. Patterns emerge and eventually become clear. You start to figure out what makes John always hit the ball better than Justin, or Sean, or Jarred.

Over time, what emerges is a clear practical understanding of good hitting. That's right, you heard me correctly: I'm saying I've discovered the secrets to great hitting and they are about to be revealed to you. This is no complicated, intellectual hitting theory. It's common sense, practical knowledge and a simple system that just works — whether you're only six or a college superstar. I've seen this again and again.

The whole purpose of this book is to do a better job teaching real people like you how to hit better. That's why it contains so many down-to-earth drills and exercises. You'll find a specific drill to lead you through any element, each step of the way. Some are the first of their kind.

Among these are several new important drills to guarantee hitters finally learn how to watch the ball and keep their "head to the bat." These drills are designed to be foolproof. Remember, my drills must work, even for eight- and nine-year-olds. Instructors know what great drills do. They teach almost automatically. They can reliably train the batter to swing correctly, even if he doesn't understand why. Each drill in this book has been carefully selected with this in mind. They have all been proven to work day in and day out, with hundreds of students.

Also included in this book are lots of special coaching tips and hints. Many little inside tricks and gimmicks that, taken all together, can make big differences in your hitting and your swing.

It even contains the latest "homespun" methods. In the youth baseball community, new training ideas are constantly sprouting up. The ones that take root and "stick" are always good. They only catch on if they work very well.

In all regards, this book is about as state-of-the-art as you'll get. Because I work the front lines, there isn't much new I don't see or hear about first.

Here are some other highlights:

❏ A special shortcut approach instructors use to the quickest possible results.

❏ A "cutting edge" collection of the newest training techniques.

❏ Superb methods for dealing with fearful batters, motivating performance, and handling failure.

The "WIN" System

My hitting formula is called the "WIN" system. It helps you do that as a hitter. Also the word "WIN" creates a simple way to remember its three guiding principles. It's an acronym. Each letter in "WIN" corresponds to a phrase covering a principle I'll give you the speech I tell many of my students: "There are only three main things you need to do to become a really good hitter. To be a good hitter you need to know how to "WIN," "W"-"I"-"N" Each letter in the word "WIN" stands for one of them. Here they are:

W: Watch the ball to the bat

I: In front of the body contact

N: No uphill swings

Hard to believe that this is about all there is to hitting well, but it's absolutely true. I've seen it work with real people in the real world, over and over, again and again. On the other hand, the formula is simple, but mastering its three components is anything but.

Achieving the three principles requires lots of quality practice time on specific drills. If you work hard enough you will see real improvement in your hitting. I know that from experience. That's the whole reason I wrote this book. I want to give real people the better tools they need to actually get better. In my, job I have to know what gets results. Now you can too.

Fast Track, Shortcut Option

People are naturally impatient. Especially when they are paying out their hard-earned money. That's why most good hitting instructors use a shortcut to speed up improvement. Normally, we take the existing swing of a player and fix its flaws, instead of rebuilding everything. Usually this will give the batter the quickest improvement with the least disruption of his performance in actual games.

On the next page is a road map for this fix-it approach. This is a quick read on the raw essentials. You can choose to read the entire book or take this fast track and fill in the rest later.

Table 1.1. Reference table for short-cuts

	Subject	Page(s)	Objective	Key photos
1.	WIN-system	11	Know guiding principles	
2.	Squared-up and square-up	27, 29	Get close to ideal set-up	3.1, 3.5
3.	Dead hands, dead hands CPR, load your gun	90	Eliminate dead hands and get loading	
4.	Hitch breaker	30, 31, 84, 85	Stop any hitching when you load	
5.	Uppercut breaker	67	Stop uppercutting	6.3
6.	Spotlight drill	78	Get 100% rotation	8.3–8.5
7.	Barrier drill	81–82	Maximize bat speed and quickness	8.6–8.8
8.	Seeing ball	36–41, 45	Really see the ball to the bat	4.11
9.	The secret of timing	69	Hit consistently "OIF"	7.8–7.10
10.	Conclusions	125	Overall focus	

2.

The Preliminaries

As a batting instructor, I work in a virtual forest of trendy bats. I get to see swing and watch perform virtually every manner and type of bat on the planet, including wood. I'll tell you the inside story on choosing correctly.

Choosing a Bat

In these high-tech times, it's easy to get caught up in the concept that a special bat will enhance your performance a lot. Of course, bat companies are hoping you will. You prob-

Fig. 2.1. With all the choices available today, you'll want to choose your bat intelligently.

ably know what I'm going to say about this hype, even if you don't want to hear it. It's still the batter and his swing that really matters, not the bat.

There are however two characteristics you need to decide on intelligently: weight and length. Ironically, for young kids, eight and under, the decision on weight is really easy, because in reality there isn't one. Having seen so many youngsters, I can tell you that the "holding the bat straight out in one hand for ten seconds test" to see if the bat is light enough is a wasted ten seconds. I've seen thousands of kids, and the simple fact is that for 90% of the youngest ones, you can't have a bat that is light enough. Just buy the lightest legal bat

Fig. 2.2. This popular "hold-it-out" test is highly overrated.

you can find, because even that will still be too heavy, and they'll be lugging it through the strike zone no matter what. I know what I'm talking about.

Table 2.1. Bat selection table

Slanting factors	Slow bat, slight ——— fast bat, strong			Slow bat, slight ——— fast bat, strong		
Age	**Bat weight (oz.)**			**Bat length (in.)**		
Under 9	The very lightest by rule			26	27	28
9–12	–12	–10	–8, –7	29	30, 31	32
13–14	–10	–8, –7	–5, –3	31	32, 33	34
High school/ College	Lightest by rule			32	33	34

An experienced educated eye can spot a bat that's dragging a hundred feet away.

If your kid is exceptionally strong, or a little older, nine and up, there might actually be a decision to be made. The hold-it-out tests just sound good, but mean nothing. It is always bat head speed that matters most for hitting. The real test is to give the prospective choices an extended swinging workout, from lightest to heavier, with rest breaks in between, and just closely watch the bat speed. You can then determine at what weight the bat whip and hop start to sag. That will help you find a good weight; just err on the light side a little.

As regards length, which is less critical than weight, it's not like this is rocket science or anything. Table 2-1 on page 16 is a chart showing typical choices by age and factors that can slant the choice one way or the other. Bat weights are traditionally expressed by listing how many ounces less than length they are.

Note:

The slow or fast bat factor is about the fact that some kids are a lot quicker and more athletic than others. Some swing quick bats, others do not. Just observe other peer kids, and trust your gut appraisal.

The main age group where options start to matter is between nine and twelve. Between these ages, batters can actually handle the different sizes and weights effectively and start to hit the ball hard enough for material and construction to make a difference. Here's the inside story on the interesting decisions to be made.

Hyperlite Versus Thicker Wall

The lightest bats — minus twelve's — employ very thin wall construction. For many kids, this doesn't really matter because they don't really hit the ball all that hard. For those who truly pound the ball, you want to avoid the hyperlites. They go dead quicker.

All metal bats are subject to metal fatigue, and power hitters get less pop from these, particularly when you hit the ball on any other than the sweet spot. I personally know of some instances where these bats were dented by the ball. If you're truly a power guy and like one of these, better plan on replacing it about once a month. I would avoid them entirely if you are a power hitter. Please don't kid yourself being macho. These bats are superb and increase performance for typical hitters, especially lighter-build ones.

Big Barrel Versus Regular

At present, this is a big issue, pun intended, for Pony and other non Little League organizations. Little League prohibits big barrels until advanced Junior and Senior levels — league age 13 and up. Other organizations, like Pony Baseball, do not. If choosing between a big barrel and a regular barrel "on your plate," here's what to consider before digging in:

Realize that you have to hit the ball with the middle part of your bat anyway. No matter what the circumference, if you don't put the middle inch or so of your bat on the ball, it will be a pop-up or weak grounder anyway. Difference in size really means nothing because you have to hit with the middle of either bat to get base hits. At its largest, the difference in diameter for a big barrel is only one half inch, or a scant quarter of an inch on each side of the bat's middle. Bottom line, it's not trivial size differences that you should care about here.

Care about these characteristics that actually matter. In theory, the advantage of a big barrel is an increased trampoline effect off the bat's surface that can increase the force of your hit. On the other hand, big barrels always weigh more. For youth league players, generally around four or five ounces more, and as much as nine. The key consideration becomes whether you are strong enough to swing a big barrel and a small barrel of equal length at virtually the same velocity. If indeed you can, the big barrel is an obvious choice, and will supply more "pop." That's a huge "if" though. If you lie to yourself, your performance will absolutely suffer, and often by lots. More often than not, the increased bat speed of a regular barrel will dwarf any slight increase in "bounce" you get from a big barrel. Try to keep your ego in check and get real, one way or the other. My advice is to have a third person give you an unbiased appraisal regarding your bat speed trials before you decide.

Loud Versus Quiet

Certain aluminum bats emit a lot louder and more distinctive sound than others. One company in particular is notorious for bats that ring and ping loudly when you hit with them. This is not an endorsement, but loud ringy bats are great to practice with, use off a tee, or for soft toss, etc. They give the batters immediate auditory feedback on how well the ball was struck by tone and sound. You can really tell easily when you hit it pure just by the sound.

Metal of the Month

It may only seem like this, but new metals and technologies seem to spring up like flavors of the month or something. The point is, companies are always trying to promote some new innovation as revolutionary, improved, or better than ever. It turns out this may or may not be the case at all.

I am familiar with several instances where products and alloys hitting the real world don't measure up to their advance billing. This is often confirmed by rapid subsequent redesign to correct some glaring problem, like cracking, for example. It's obvious to me that the real world is much different than the laboratory. You may want to consult with the "word on the street" before your purchase. High school baseball team kids are always plugged in here, and are a worthwhile source for blunt appraisals on products, characteristics, and brands.

In my experience, some of the older alloys outperform and stay "live" longer than many of their newer buddies — and by lots. If you're not made of money, you'll want an alloy that keeps its pop. When my customers ask my advice on what bat they should buy this is my normal reasoning:

First, I factor in the kid's build and bat speed. Then I almost always suggest a bat that is an inch longer and an ounce heavier than I feel would be perfect. That way, they can expect to use the bat at least two seasons. Unless you've just got money burning a hole in your pocket, it makes sense to do likewise. You can choke up an inch, which makes the bat swing an ounce lighter for a while, and grow into it. I highly recommend this practical approach. In any case, don't ever fall for the idea you need a new bat just because the maker says their latest alloy is so much better. I've found many times it's just the opposite.

Sting Stoppers

Some bats boast all kinds of construction to reduce the vibration and sting caused by miss hits near the hands and end cap. All I can tell you is that whatever difference is achieved, you can't tell it by the faces of my students. When they get jammed by a ball near their hands, they still get the same pained expression, and shake and rub their hands and fingers like usual. For some reason, the saying "back to the drawing board" seems appropriate. Seriously, there is all this effort to prevent stinging. Even if it could be done, it wouldn't be a good idea. Try hitting the ball on the sweet spot. From my perspective, getting a little sting when your timing is faulty is poetic justice. I look at it as a perfect punishment, which hopefully should encourage you to improve your timing in your next swing.

Wood Versus Metal

There are always periodic revival movements for wooden bats in youth leagues. Wooden bats definitely have an eternal appeal. They still emit a wonderful "crack of the bat" whenever you get a ball on the sweet spot. The thing is, that won't happen nearly as much with a wooden bat as it will with a metal counterpart. Metal bats have much larger and more forgiving sweet spots. They hit the ball harder. Most importantly, they are a lot lighter. Many kids are not strong enough to swing properly with metal, let alone wood. From my perspective, kids have enough trouble swinging correctly as it is. For my part, I wouldn't recommend making it harder.

3.

Getting Started

First and foremost, it's vital that you understand there is an ideal swing. Here's a brief history lesson to explain why you might not know this, or want to accept it. Historically, in baseball, no one really paid much attention to the science and physics of the swing, or even common sense.

For years, the guiding principle was to build a "natural" swing around whatever felt good to you. In reality, this was an ignorance is bliss thing. At the time, it made lots of batters feel really good, special, and unique. With no evidence to the contrary, they could go around telling

Fig. 3,1. A perfect set-up makes it easiest to hit.

Fig. 3.2. Open stance.

anyone who would listen why their swing and its theory was the real deal. For years, the hitting theory was closer to magic than science. In a game full of legend and myth, few wanted to hear anything about one set of swing mechanics that makes it easiest to hit the ball hard and solid. Okay, that was the past,

Fig. 3.3. Square stance.

Fig. 3.4. Close stance.

and this in now. Get over it. It is absolute fact that there is an ideal swing. Indeed, one set of swing mechanics that makes it easiest to hit the ball hard and solid. You need to realize that to hit your best, you must learn this swing — no matter how good you think you're hitting now. If you go around to almost any high school or college these days and watch their baseball hitters, you will see an interesting confirmation of this. The swings of the batters will look extremely similar. The set-up positions will undoubtedly be closer to identical. Now we know better — there is a simple reason for this: There is an ideal swing. Learn it, use it, or lose it.

The "Set-Up"— Foundation for Success

The more perfect your set-up, the better your swing. It's the base everything starts from. I can tell you that everything good or bad flows out of your set up. It's a lot like when you learn to play a musical instrument. If you don't start out in the correct position, it's about impossible to make music. In batting, everything about a perfect set up is intended to make your swing as short, simple, and easy as possible. Believe me, hitting a baseball thrown at great velocity is definitely one of the most difficult things in all of sports. When you are trying "to put a round bat, on a round ball—squarely" everything you can do to make that easier is a big deal.

Foot Placement

Your stance should be mostly square. Figs. 3.2, 3.3 and 3.4 show the three common stances for your feet. For hitters just starting out, you can't go wrong with completely square. It is very common for youngsters to tend to be late swinging at the ball. Often, one of the main reasons for this is a front foot that is too "closed," too much out ahead of the rear foot. This can restrict a proper hip turn by in essence getting the front leg in the way of the turn. Avoid any extreme foot positions entirely. Moderation is the key. If a player really feels he must open or close his stance, it should be only a little.

Set your feet a few inches wider than your shoulders. This way you will be able to get a strong weight shift with only a short stride (see Fig. 3.1).

Rear Foot Pivot

"Pigeon toe" your rear foot. Make sure your rear toe points inward, toward the middle of your body somewhat (see Fig. 3.5). This speeds up the complete turning of your hips that you want, by letting your rear foot pivot and spin up faster. This rear foot pivot feels like how you might mash a pesky bug by twisting your toe on top of it — only really fast, like mashing a bug. This crucial spinning up on the toe of your rear foot is what allows you to rapidly rotate your hips and knees properly, so they end up facing the pitcher (see Fig. 3.6). Most of your power comes from this "turning on the ball." You need to really "fire" your rear foot pivot for an explosive swing.

Center your weight a little more toward your back foot and slightly more toward the balls of your feet. This makes weight shifting quickest. You will see that quickness is a constant theme when it comes to good hitting.

Above: Fig. 3.5. Pointing your rear foot inward like this will speed up your hip turn.

Below: Fig. 3.6. The rear foot pivot feels like twisting your toe on a bug to "mash" it.

Coaching Tip: "Time Flies"

Each of these small details in the stance matters. Batters often have less than half a second to swing. Every tiny part of a second matters. Consider this fact. It's really hard to believe, but true. With the fastest pitchers in pro, or little league, the difference between a late foul ball or a ball somewhere fair is only one hundredth of a second late.

Fig. 3.7. Basically, the second knuckles of both hands should line up.

Above: Fig. 3.8. Pieces of tape can speed learning a correct grip.

Below: Fig. 3.9. If you don't wear gloves, use a marker or black electrical tape instead.

Grip

Basically, your second (middle) knuckles line up (see Fig. 3.7). The second knuckles on your top hand should always be somewhere between the first and second knuckles on your bottom hand. Beware of lining up your first knuckles. For some reason this "choke grip" is common among very young kids. Watch out for this one. It hurts bat speed and promotes uppercutting. Change it pronto.

Coaching Tip: "The Tape Marks the Way"

To master the right grip quickly, put pieces of tape on a finger of each glove that line up when the grip is correct. If you don't wear gloves, use easy erase marker (see Figs. 3.8 and 3.9).

Grip Pressure

The key is to always grip only as hard as necessary for control. Start with a fairly relaxed grip, but grip with smoothly increasing force to maintain control. As the bat accelerates near impact, squeeze tightly and press hard into the ball. You really won't have to think about this part. To hang onto your speeding and colliding bat, you will instinctively grip like crazy. This dynamic gripping creates the most explosive wrist and bat whip while still letting you control your bat.

Coaching Tip: "Fingers Rule"

Grip the bat somewhat more in the fingers than the palm. This increases bat speed similar to the way it increases ball speed for a pitcher when he holds the ball in his fingers rather than his palm.

Body Alignment

The key is a simple, fairly erect posture (see Figs. 3.10 and 3.11). Just be sure to flex your knees somewhat to make the weight shift and hip turn easy. Try turning your hips stiff-legged so you'll understand.

Fig. 3.10. Correct upright posture (front view).

Fig. 3.11. Correct upright posture (rear view).

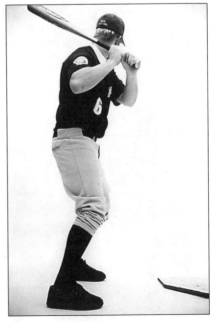

Overall, you want to start and stay relatively "tall" with only moderate flex. Then, your body segments stack right over each other and balance very naturally. Bend only a little at the waist. Your relatively compact upright center of gravity allows the most explosive rotation, and the stillest head.

Don't crouch, lean, or bend way over (see Fig. 3.13). These are swing wreckers, forcing extra movement for no reason. Many crouchers and leaners "stand up" as they swing, which moves the head and eyes all over the place. Your ideal swing is much simpler, as simple as possible, with the fewest adjustments and the least to go wrong.

A mostly upright posture gives you the quickest rotation, best balance, and a still head.

"Squared-Up" Position of the Hands and Elbows

At set-up, you want to position your hands right near the top of the strike zone by your rear shoulder. It's common sense. This sets up the easiest, simplest, shortest way to hit strikes and still use gravity for help. The top of your top hand should just touch a line at the shoulders. Both elbows should be square and even, hanging comfortably downward. This is called "squared-up." (See Figs. 3.12 and 3.7). Notice how everything fits squarely into a nice tidy imaginary rectangle square to the ground. Take note how the front arm is bent considerably at set up. It should always form the kind of reverse "L' depicted. An overly stiff, straightened out front arm will

Fig. 3.13. Don't crouch, lean or bend way over like this.

make your swing much longer and slower to the ball.

"But That's Not What My Favorite Pro Does"

It's common for batters to decide to copy their favorite professional hitters. This can often be disastrous in terms of a horrible set-up far removed from the ideal squared-up position. Don't walk stupidly into this killer trap. Understand the facts.

Many professional hitters were unaware of ideal techniques when they developed their swings. There's no other way to say this. Lots of pros have ended up with crappy swings with all kinds of flaws. The only reason some of them work at all is the sheer greatness of the athlete holding the bat. The problem is, all these swings, bad or not, are now totally "grooved" by literally millions of repetitions. Mo Vaughn for example has a gigantic hitch in his swing. Should you copy one of those? Only if you're an idiot, and think you can somehow defy the laws of physics.

So why don't the pros change? Simply put, pros are reluctant to ever risk changing their swings in the slightest, let alone in a major way, when it could jeopardize their delicate timing and cost them millions. It may sound a little funny and ironic, but you don't have that problem. You can afford to do it right.

Try Knowing What You're Looking At

Whenever you analyze anyone swinging, especially professionals, it helps to know what you're really seeing. Here are some tips on how.

Hopefully you can avoid making some stupid mistake copying something you only think you see. Understand that there are three distinct phases to take a look at early in the swing. These are the phases of set-up, load, and launch. Would be copycats usually are preoccupied with the position of the hands, so for the moment we'll talk only about hand position during the three phases. First is the set-up. Amongst the pros, it is possible to see all kinds of wild set-up positions for the hands not even remotely close to what the correct squared-up position prescribes. That's the trap. Copycats take notice of only that positioning. Now they somehow feel all they need to do is copy that hand position and they'll hit great.

It's pretty clear that they don't understand the next phase. If they did, they would likely give up copying for good. During the next phase, called the load, when the hands draw back to cock the bat, every good hitter on the planet moves his hands into an almost identical position right near, and somewhat in back of, the rear shoulder at the top of the strike zone. It is from this position that almost all good hitters launch their hands forward to the ball.

What a revelation. No matter how weird and wild the set-up positions, good hitters all load to and launch from nearly the same position. The squared-up set-up position is just the logical improvement over any other wild one you might want to copy. This is because the set-up, load, and launch positions for the hands are all simply and efficiently as

close together as possible. Anyone with common sense can appreciate how this just makes it easiest to hit. Simple, easy, uncomplicated. You will see these themes about the ideal swing constantly repeated in this book.

Master Coaching Tip: "Squared-Up" Shortcut

Get near perfect by simply placing the bat on your shoulder and then just lift your hands slightly. I usually have kids make it a habit to tap the bat on their shoulder, and then lift, before every swing. Use this to speed learning.

Coaching Tip: "Taking Dead Aim"

Try aiming your front forearm and elbow like a gun sight. You should feel like it's aiming right toward the middle of the contact zone, out in front of your hip, for the perfect belt-high strike. You're now "locked and loaded" to "shoot" your hands straight on target. Take dead aim with your forearm "sight" and you'll get great results (see Fig. 3.1).

Common "Squared-Up" Disasters

Hands too high:

You want your hands down close to the zone. Lots of batters seem to like their hands far too high above their back shoulder. This is poor technique. It will result in one of two undesirable things: You will have to hitch your hands down as you load to get back down to the proper launch position, or worse, you will just launch down on a steep angle from too high a position. This not only makes contact harder, it encourages uppercutting as well. Lots of youngsters are drawn to a high hand position. Using gravity to jump start their bats is tempting because it's easier than good technique. Don't fall for this lazy substitute. You'll never hit your best (see Fig. 3.14).

Fig. 3.14. Hands way too high and too far away from the striking zone.

Fig. 3.15. Never "fly" your back elbow up like this.

Hitching:

Once you've got your hands in the proper squared-up position, right at or slightly below shoulder height, don't blow it by moving them down and up and all around during the loading phase. This is known as hitching. To load right you have to always cock your hands almost straight back. Never dance them, down and then up before launch. This hitching often feels very good, but so does upper-

cutting. You don't want either. A hitch complicates and slows your swing by adding lots of unnecessary movement. Hitchers often get caught late somewhere in the middle of their hitch instead of the launch position. Naturally, that makes it hard to hit, particularly with any consistency. If that were not enough, it also contributes to uppercutting because hitchers often end up dropping their hands down below high strikes. See also "coiling" in chapter 8.

Back Elbow Up:

Fig. 3.16. The back elbow gets tucked and locked to the torso for power.

Never "fly" your back elbow. It gets tucked and locked to your torso. A short connection lets you generate power quickest. Anything that slows and complicates this crucial connection is a serious mistake (see Figs. 3.15 and 3.16). "Getting the back arm up" as they say is the single biggest hitting myth that just won't die. Never mind the fact that it's entirely wrong. It has a life of it's own. Maybe we can finally put it to rest here. For starters, realize that no expert hitting instructor even recommends it. It's not in any hitting book I've ever seen.

That should tell you something. A myth is an idea that is commonly perceived to be true, but isn't. All that "flying your elbow" does is fly in the face of common sense. It's wrong. It slows your swing. It slows the critical power connection between the back elbow and the torso. Don't do it. RIP, baby!

Starting "Close"

This phrase refers to how close or far away from your body you want to carry your hands at set-up and later at launch. It's important because if your hands are held too far away from the torso, you lose power and the ability to rotate your quickest. If they're too tight, you can't jerk them around in front of your body quickly

Top left: Fig. 3.17. Shake hands with top hand.

Bottom left: Fig. 3.18. Pivot up to shoulder height.

Below right: Fig. 3.18. Grip with bottom hand.

enough to pull the fat part of the bat in to hit a hard inside pitch — what is known as "getting around on an inside pitch" or "shortening up." You could say, your body can get in the way if they're too tight.

At set-up you want to position your hands fairly close to your body, so long as you have absolutely no feeling whatsoever of being scrunched in. What you're after is best described as close, yet comfortable (see Fig. 3.20). The following coaching tip will help you get a pretty good feel for this.

you're driving your hands with your entire body from the bottom of your toes to the top of your shoulders. If you don't feel a smooth, powerful connection, try adjusting your close hands position until you do.

When you find this ideal close hand position you create a very powerful, body-driven stroke.

Coaching Tip: "Shake On It"

Stand like shaking hands, upper arm straight at your side. Then, just pivot your hand up to shoulder height to locate a fairly correct top hand position (see Figs. 3.17, 3.18 and 3.19).

You always want your hands to synchronize and move with your entire body in unison. This way you harness your entire body and the large muscles of your legs and torso to start, cock, and accelerate the bat. When it's right, it feels like

Fig. 3.20. Hands are held close but never scrunched up.

Bat Angle

The vertical angle of the bat, catcher's view, should be close to forty five degrees, but never greater (see Fig. 3.11). Higher angles make the bat head loop and travel further, slowing your swing. This angle helps promote a more horizontal sideways attack on the ball that is important to help you maximize contact.

Balance

Get balance by rehearsing a "feeling." Your goal is to be like a cat ready to pounce, "firm on the ground, but ready to spring." Practice this feeling whenever you warm up. If you ever loose your balance, remember: "firm on the ground, but ready to spring." You won't believe how well this works.

Coaching Tip: "Flying Blind"

An effective way to work on your balance is by simply closing your eyes. This automatically sharpens your feel for balance, or for other things:

swinging level, weight shifting, etc. Incorporate this technique and try using it part of the time when you warm up or work on drills.

Head Position

You must always keep both eyes on the ball to have depth perception.

At set-up, turn your head as far as possible toward the pitcher. Make sure you keep both eyes on the pitcher when you load and cock back your bat. This small backward turn can easily pull your back eye off the ball. Make sure that won't happen by always turn-

Fig. 3.21. Looks strange but works great for learning head positioning.

ing your head fully toward the pitcher to begin with.

Coaching Tip: "The Bite That's Right"

Turn your head completely and then bite your shirt on the front shoulder. This sort of holds your head in place and will definitely remind you to get into proper head positioning. You can quit when you're sure the correct habits have taken (see Fig. 3.21).

Top left: Fig. 3.22. Holding your head straight will force your eyes to move more.

Bottom left: Fig. 3.23. Pre-tilting your head will reduce movement.

Bottom right: Fig. 3.24. Now your head will swivel only on one plane.

Getting That Special Best Look

Many experts tell you to keep your head completely level at set-up (see Fig. 3.22). I strongly disagree. The fact is you have to tilt your head and eyes slightly down to properly watch the ball to the bat, known as "head to the bat."

It makes a lot more sense to set up with your head already in this slightly tilted position (see Fig. 3.23). That way, you can now simply and smoothly pivot your head on one plane, to look the ball into your bat (see Fig. 3.24). Many pros do it. This slight pre tilt allows your head and eyes remain quieter, giving you the best possible look at the ball.

4.

Master Secret No. 1: Learning to Really Watch the Ball

Everything about hitting depends on "seeing the ball." "If you don't see the ball, you can't hit it" is one of the oldest and wisest sayings in baseball. Yet, this is a difficult skill that is too often taken for granted. Few books discuss it. It seems everyone thinks you automatically see the ball, so why bother, right? Easy as can be. Actually, you're about to find out why nothing could be further from the truth.

Pulling Your "Head"

Hitters need to watch and track the ball as close to impact as possible (see Fig. 4.1). It's difficult. There are two main problems. The first is called "pulling your head." You've heard the expression "I can't wait to see that." Well, that is literally what happens at bat, over and over again. Hitters pull their eyes up off the ball early, often well before impact, because they are so anxious and excited to see where it goes. You could say they can't wait (see Fig. 4.2).

This is a natural human reflex, and it never goes away. Ask any golfer. It turns out that the number one flaw that plagues hitters is pulling their heads.

"Peaking"

There is a second common and serious "seeing the ball" problem called "peaking." This is exactly what you think it is. Instead of turning your head toward the ball as it gets closer to keep your eyes directly facing the ball, many hitters, especially young ones, move only their eyes and peak at the ball. You can always spot a peaker by specifically watching their nose. If the nose stays up and does not turn down and toward the bat near the contact point, that hitter is peaking at the ball. I see the worst possible scenario all the time: batters who peak and pull their heads as well.

Coaching Tip: "Want the Good or the Bad News First?"

The bad news: unlike any other physical batting skill, watching the ball to the bat you can never really master at all. You will have to constantly battle and work on it for as long as you play. The basic human curiosity, urge, and reflex to look up early never lessens.

The good news: now you know it, you can decide to work on it constantly.

Master Coaching Tip: "Keep Your Nose on the Ball"

Practice keeping your nose pointing directly at the ball until it hits the bat. This single drill combats both head pulling and "peaking." Coaches, try telling your hitters, "keep your nose on the ball" and "stick your nose on the hit" constantly.

Batters must understand the enemies they are up against. These are strong instinctual forces at work here, virtually reflexes. It is not natural or easy for any human being to turn his face toward a speeding object being hurled toward them. In fact, it's just the opposite. There can be no doubt of this when you study very young children totally new to the sport. There is always a natural innate fear response you're dealing with. Hopefully, this

will help you appreciate why watching the ball is a much more difficult skill than most people think. It is extremely important to work relentlessly on it if you expect to be any kind of a good hitter.

The "W" in the "WIN" System: Watch The Ball to the Bat

The first principle of great hitting is the big "W" in the "WIN" method. Watch the ball all the way to the bat, every time. It's called "head to the bat" (see Fig. 4.1). I would prefer you think of it as "nose to the bat." Either way here's what it is about. The best hitters start out looking at the pitcher, but always end up looking down at the bat at contact

Above: Fig. 4.1. Pulling your head is when you look up early, often way before contact.
Below: Fig. 4.2. Head to the bat — I like to think of it as "nose to the bat."

The Challenge

Watch any unsuspecting player hit off a batting tee. Get a really good look at his eyes. Virtually every player will "pull" his head and start looking up before the bat makes contact.

Want another eye opener? Pun intended. Play catch with

any player. Really observe just how closely he watches and follows the ball. Without doubt, he will be very lazy tracking the ball. The typical player will only peak or glance vaguely in its general direction, particularly over the last few feet.

To hit or even catch your best in baseball you need to really watch the ball, not just glance or peak at it. Here's how you can learn the specific ball watching skills, crucial for your best hitting performance.

First-Aid Ball Watching 101

Baby Step One: "Nose Catch"

It's tremendously important to track the ball by moving your entire head, not just your eyes. It's ironic, but the best way to start improving your hitting is by playing a special kind of catch, rather than by batting. Here's how. Anytime you play catch, especially every pre-game or practice warm-up, concentrate on keeping your nose pointing directly at the ball all the way into your glove.

Make sure you always catch the ball well "out in front" of the body, arms extended. Keep your nose locked on the ball from the moment of release until it enters your glove or hands (see Figs. 4.3, 4.4 and 4.5). Do it bare hand first and get the hang of it before using gloves. Start and keep doing this religiously.

Coaching Tip: "Fair Warning"

Most players do a good job "nosing" the ball into their gloves. Trouble is guys always seem to get lazy about picking up the release point. Whenever a ball is thrown to you, make it a habit to work on picking the ball up right out of the hand. This is an extremely important skill required for great hitting. Don't get lazy about practicing it.

"Out in Front, Where It's At"

Something for you to keep in mind is that great players always hit and field the ball out in front of their eyes and bodies. Explore this. Have a friend

Above: Fig. 4.3. Nose catch ready position.

Below: Fig. 4.4. Nose catch out in front.

toss a ball at your chest. First catch it very close in to your chest. Notice how far and fast your head has to move to properly keep your nose on the ball. Now, "nose catch" the same toss well out in front of your chest with your arms extended (see Fig. 4.4).

Understand the difference. You "see" the second toss much better because your head doesn't have to move nearly as much. That's why "out in front" is so important. It gives you the best vision that is cru-

Fig. 4.5. Nose catch trains you to track the ball by moving your entire head.

cial for both hitting and fielding.

In lessons, I "hammer" the importance of "out in front" this way: First, I have the batter stare out and lock his eyes on the pitcher. Then I hold up a first ball right out over the plate in front of his belly button. He then turns his head to look at this ball, paying attention to just how far his head moved. Once again, he stares at the pitcher. Now I hold a ball a foot out in front of his hip out near the desired contact position. Of course, when he looks at this ball, his head moves only a little. This is the critical difference between great vision and something less. The difference between seeing a speeding ball perfectly or watching a fuzzy blur. Trust me, "out in front" is absolutely positively "where it's at."

Baby Step Two: "Bat Catch"

This is the same idea as nose catch, but now you assume your batting stance, without a bat. Have a thrower now toss over the plate just like you were hitting. Simply swing your hands out as if batting, but catch the ball. Make sure your catch occurs somewhere out in front of your hip in the ideal contact area for hitting. Again, concentrate on keeping your nose on the ball and watching it all the way into your hands. Do bare hand and with gloves. In reality, you are now practicing your hitting — watching the ball to the bat and putting your nose on the contact. Your hands or gloves just substitute for your bat. Remember, nose on release point, nose on ball, nose on catch, and "out in front" (see Figs. 4.6 and 4.7).

Practicing Head to the Bat

Here's a complete routine for practicing to keep your "nose on the ball." See it all the way to the bat, and never pull your head before contact. do some or all of these every batting practice session.

1. Take some pitches. Just keep your nose on the ball from release to all the way into the catchers glove.

Above: Fig. 4.6. Ready position for bat catch.
Below: Fig. 4.7. Swing your hands out like hitting, but catch the ball instead.

2. Hands only swings, with pitcher or machine throwing over the plate as usual. Just clasp your hands together and back off the plate so you won't get hit. Take strong cuts with nose on imagined contact (see Figs. 4.8 and 4.9). Realize how easy it is to keep your head in when no ball is hit to tempt you to look up. The message: "nose on contact" will be easy if only I have discipline.

3. Make several bunts. Watch the ball hit the bat (see Fig. 4.10). If the bat has graphics, see which one it hits. Bunting is the easiest way to practice seeing the ball to the bat. Your urge to see where the ball goes is smaller.

Coaching Tip: "Wake Up and Smell the Coffee"

Bunting shows you how it's possible to virtually see contact. Realize that it is attainable every time, whether swinging or bunting.

Coaching Tip: "Catchy" Bunting Magic

Imagine a small ball-sized glove glued right on the sweet spot of your bat, or a large protruding nail. Assume a correct bunt stance (see Fig. 4.11). Now just concentrate on the idea of "catching" the ball softy in your visualized "glove" or on your imaginary "nail" The best bunters don't hit bunts, they gently catch them. Keep the bat angled up. Don't drop the bat

Figs. 4.8. and 4.9. Watching the ball all the way is easy when you know there won't be a hit ball to watch.

Fig. 4.10. Batter sticks his nose on the bunt contact.

head down with your hands. Always bring it down correctly by only bending your knees. It also helps to work on bunting the top half of the ball.

4. Check swings. Check swing some pitches. Because you hold up your swing around contact it's easier to tell if you're seeing the ball hit the bat. This is a great way to gradually dial in your timing. Start out almost bunting, but check up less and

Fig. 4.11. Correct bunt stance: bat is well out in front.

less. All the while working on head work.

5. "Watch it disappear" drill, super star maker. When you swing, try to actually watch the ball hit your bat. At impact, don't look up to see where it goes. Instead, rivet your eyes and nose to the contact point, and watch the ball "disappear." The instant after contact, force yourself to look down at a spot on the ground, instead of up to see where the ball goes. This is unbelievably effective because you are practicing the exact opposite of pulling your head (see Fig. 4.12).

6. The "three" drill for batting practice. As you hit, work only on getting your "best look," and nothing else. After each swing, without being asked, tell your coach a number from one to three indicating how well you saw the ball. Three is perfect, two is okay, one is . This drill sharpens your "best look." You'll soon see that your best hits are almost always threes.

Note:

It is entirely possible to get a three look and still miss the ball. When this happens, I like to ask the batter whether the ball went under or over his bat. A confident correct answer confirms he's doing a good job in spite of any miss.

Master Coaching Tip: "On the Nose"

The nose always tells if a batter really watched a ball to his bat. If it turns down toward contact then he did, if it doesn't, he didn't (see Figs. 4.1 and 4.2).

Coaches: Look for this. Make a habit of instructing, "Stick your nose on the contact."

Fig. 4.12. Batter watches the ball disappear and looks at the ground instead of following the hit ball.

47

Coaching Tip: "Too Much Of a Good Thing"

Do steps five and six in moderation. Let players watch at least half their hits if they want.

7. Optional lucky number 7: "Net Catch." This drill is without equal. It is optional because you must buy a fish net, or make one from a tennis racket and garden shade fabric. You pitch light-weight balls, and the batter simply swings, catches, and stares them into the net (see Fig. 4.13). Start with several check swings. You will be amazed just how much easier it is to watch the ball in when you know it's not going anywhere. This seldom fails to get batters to execute successfully, keeping their nose on the ball all the way.

Lightning in a Bottle: The "Cut It in Half" Gimmick

A "gimmick" is a simple idea that "tricks" you into performing difficult tasks automatically, especially under pressure. The "cut it in half" gimmick is the greatest of all hitting gimmicks.

The idea is simple. Every time you swing, try to "cut the ball exactly in half." If you're looking at a ball to pick out its center, you're certain to be looking at the ball! This gimmick is amazing. It makes you perform, by seeing the ball well, no matter what. It requires so much concentration, there isn't much time to experience pressure or distracting negative thoughts. This insulates you from pres-

Fig. 4.13. Net catch is a fail-proof way to learn nose to the bat.

Figs. 4.14 (above) and 4.15 (below). You need to practice keeping your head still by swinging "shoulder to shoulder."

sure. That's huge. Coaches, say this often in games and practice (see also page 120, "Sole Swing Thoughts").

Related Drills "Shoulder To Shoulder" Drill

You need to practice a still head. This will require that you practice making swings where your chin starts on the front shoulder and ends up on the back one, while your head stays put. Practice moving only your shoulders, not your head (see Figs. 4.14 and 4.15). Commonly, the rear shoulder can knock the head out, preventing you from properly watching the contact. The remedy is to swing very slowly and make corrections. Then patiently speed up to normal.

Hint:

many problems stem from too vertical a swing with an overly high follow-through. There are way too many would-be golfers out there. A more side-to-side swing with a flat follow through, just barely at the shoulders, will often help eliminate this problem.

"Pepper Drill"

Check swing pepper games (see page 105) are great for head-to-the-bat work (see Fig. 4.16) Just make sure it's "nose on contact" pepper where the batter is "out" if he pulls his head. Be sure to enforce this.

"Spin Drill"

For younger batters and slow pitch speeds, it works as follows: A batter must show a

coach exactly how the ball was spinning right at impact, with his finger. While you're busy seeing spin, you can't help

Above: Fig. 4.17. Watching the contact on the twang.

Left: Fig. 4.16. Check swing "pepper" is a great way to practice head to the bat.

watching the ball in the process.

Coaching Tip: "The Twang, Head Trainer Deluxe"

Get a two-foot piece of garden hose. Tie the hose on a chain link fence belt-high so one end sticks out a foot. Vise grips can help hold it. Paint an inch of the tip. It's done. Always start the drill by looking out at an imaginary pitcher. Now imagine tracking a pitch that ends up right at the tip. Swing at the target, riveting your eyes to the contact. The twang even sharpens your aim, being only an inch wide (see Fig. 4.17). Set up one or several of these and use them as a mandatory components for every batting practice.

5.

The Swing to the Ball

The oldest wisdom in baseball is still the best: The correct stroke is a chop with a follow-through. Chops deliver tremendous force very accurately. Like chopping trees, pounding nails, or driving railroad spikes. Like delivering a crushing blow to a speeding baseball.

What's a Chop?

Just try to drive your hands laser straight to the ball. Like they were shot from a gun. When you swing, the path of your hands only feels dead straight. The bat head itself will take a nice tight arc to the ball, leveling out perfectly, just like you want, all through the impact area (see Figs. 5.12, 5.13 and 5.14).

Note:

After you chop, always follow through fully. This is a chop swing. Start watching the very best hitters in your league or school. Notice how most of their swings will look much more linear than curvy.

Above: Fig. 5.1. Chop-swing practice ready position.

Below: The chop-swing feels a lot like a two-handed karate chop.

Coaching Tip: "The Straighter The Greater"

Remind batters to "swing straight to the ball" constantly.

Learning the Power Chop-Swing

Get in your stance, but without a bat. Now press and hold your palms firmly together. Cock them back and powerfully chop them laser straight through an imaginary pitch (see Figs. 5.1,

Fig. 5.3. The chop-swing impact would occur about here.

Above: Fig. 5.4. Chopping a sock target will develop your accuracy.

Below: Fig. 5.5. Chop-swing some sock balls

5.2 and 5.3). Like hitting it with a two handed karate chop with the front edges of both hands, always follow through normally.

Feel the simple accuracy of your chop-swing. Get a sock and mark its tip as a target. Hang it so you can chop-swing the target about belt-high (see Fig. 5.4). Later, try different heights. Practice until you can chop-swing straight and pin point, over and over.

I hesitated to cover this subject because for some people it doesn't apply. However, in seven years of coaching, I have encountered only three students who performed the straight chop too literally and ended up with a very straight overly downward bat head path through the impact zone. Kind of an uppercut problem in reverse. I mention it only because, though rare, it is possible and was difficult to correct.

The "Sock Ball" Drill

Roll socks into balls. Have someone pitch them. Hit them with your hands using your karate chop-swing (see Fig. 5.5).

Include some nose-on contact work. Next, get an old broom handle or similar rod and cut off a sixteen inch piece. Practice hitting more socks using this intentionally short stick as a bat.

Now get an actual bat. Take some chop-swings (see Fig. 5.6). If this does not feel identical to your hand chop swing, repeat the hands-only drills until it does. With a bat, work off a "T." Hit some baseballs with the identical chopping motion. Do some chop-swing soft toss.

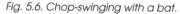

Fig. 5.6. Chop-swinging with a bat.

As you work through these steps, you'll want to check your progress toward your real objective. The ultimate prize is to reach a point where you know your bat head always follows your hands straight to any target, every time. This is pretty much worth selling your soul for. Once you forge this direct linkage, you will always have the simplest stroke and deadly accuracy. You will be on your way to being a good hitter. Maybe a great one.

Important:

See Figs. 5.7 through 5.16, hereafter known as the "core section" photographs. Notice how the bat head always stays above your hands until just before contact. This is crucial when you swing. It causes your bat head to follow the hands directly to the ball, without uppercutting.

A chopping cut through the ball will be the pillar of your great swing. With enough practice, all you'll need to hit well is chop your hands through the ball. Just like the carpenter knows he'll hit the nail. The chop-swing is the foundation

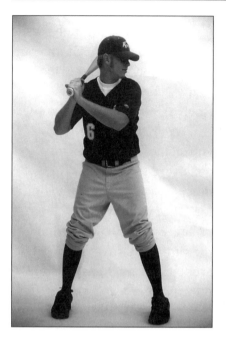

Above: Fig. 5.7. It all starts with a "squared-up" set-up.
Below: Fig. 5.8. A small backward turn cocks the bat and starts to load weight against the back feet.

Above: Fig. 5.9. The swing is fully loaded. The hip turn has cocked the knee and front foot. Below: Fig. 5.10. At launch, an explosive weight shift is begun by a hard pivot of the back foot and hips.

Above: Fig. 5.11. The back elbow now tucks to the hips for power.
Below: Fig. 5.12. As turning progresses, the hips begin to throw the hands instead of dragging them.

Above: Fig. 5.13. The bat head is now accelerating violently to catch up with the hands near impact. Below: Fig. 5.14. At impact, the bat has leveled out into a nearly perfect flat-handed hammer.

Fig. 5.15, Full extension is achieved. Note the stiff front leg characteristic of rotational hitting.

Fig. 5.16. A complete follow-through. Note how full rotation has caused the braced front foot to tilt.

for the swings of all great hitters. It always has been and always will be.

Do Not Pass "Go"— Before Passing This Test

In my lessons, students start out hitting off a batting tee. I'm always shocked, but some regularly miss the ball on the tee. If you haven't got a swing with the bat control to hit a stationary ball, you're just plain not ready to try to improve hitting a moving one.

Let a simple test decide: Make sure you can hit a hundred balls in a row off a tee before you go any farther.

Coaching Tip: "Slow Motion and Back and Forth"

Practicing in slow motion aids learning. Advanced hitters should be capable of frame-by-frame slow. It helps with many drills to begin slow, and then gradually speed up. Work backward in slow motion as well. Try this: Start out in a perfect power position impact point and then slowly reverse back right to your set-up. Then try back and forth, retracing over and over the right swing path with good mechanics. This works great to perfect your crucial level stroke through the contact zone.

Coaching Tip: "Divide and Conquer"

Break the swing into smaller parts for easier learning. Example: For the chop-swing hands drills, you might do the chop only without a follow through for a while. In fact, you might try the chop in slow motion.

Then, eyes closed. Get it? Use all the tools.

Swing Instruction For the Youngest

These phrases are nothing short of magical when it comes to teaching the basics to very little kids, age 5-plus. Just stick with them. Tell youngsters, "throw your hands straight at the ball." Repeat this constantly, along with "watch the ball all the way to your bat." There is a variation on this. Tell the kid, "Throw your bat head straight at the ball." Use both, because different kids always seem to do better with one over the other. These sayings are so good and true, they actually work well at any age, for basics at least.

6.

Master Secret No. 2: Level Swing

A level swing keeps the bat head aligned with the ball longest through the contact zone. The result is maximum contact with fewest misses — a hitter's dream. Drawing Fig. 6.1 illustrates how the ideal "level" path for your bat head promotes the most contact. Contrast this to the inherent inefficiency of the uppercut path in Fig. 6.2. Here's what makes for an ideal level swing.

A Side-to-Side, Inside-Out Cut

Your ideal level swing should always feel and be mostly side-to-side. The ideal swing is an inside-out swing. This means the hands attack the ball from inside its path. This is called keeping your hands inside the ball, and good hitters all do it. What this creates is a flatfish "sideways" rotational attack on the ball. This increases contact because it puts the bat in a relatively flat position. With a side-to-side swing more of the bat will be near to the height and plane of the incoming pitch. Contrast this to a swing that is too vertical, like a golf swing. This brings the bat through the contact area on a steeper angle that means more misses. If the ball is misjudged even a little in or out, up or down, a steeply angled bat will miss more often than a flat one. An inside-out, mostly side-to-side swing produces the most effective ideal stroke.

The "N" in the "WIN" System: No Uphill Swings

The Ideal of a Level Downswing

When you swing with a proper chop-swing, the arc of your bat resembles a famous corporate "swish" symbol (see Fig 6.1).

Note how approaching impact, this arc keeps your hands and bat head above the ball, not below. The opposite of an up-

percut. See "core section" photographs on pages 56 through 58.

This is huge: By staying above the ball entering the contact zone, you cut down on misses. Batters overwhelmingly miss by swinging under the ball on any fastball. Hitters overwhelmingly tend to be late, not early. With an ideal chop swing, your bat head will either be level with the ball or above it, but not under. This will maximize your contact by keeping you from missing under so much.

It should feel like you're swinging slightly downhill through any strike. This very slight downward cut through the impact zone is ideal, called a level downswing. This is the angle of attack that actually hits

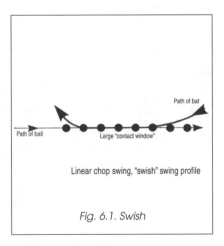

Fig. 6.1. Swish

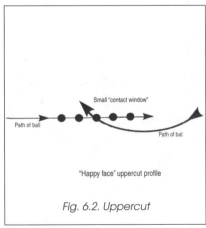

Fig. 6.2. Uppercut

driven balls and liners farther by increasing backspin and lift.

No Uphill Swings

If you never swing uphill, you'll never uppercut. You want no uphill swings. If you're swinging "down and straight out," the "swish" level downswing, with lots of line drives and hard grounders, you're on the right track, literally.

A lot about swinging level is common sense. I often hold a ball out belt high in front of my students. I tell them if they want to hit their best they'll always try to hit every pitch straight ahead. Basically, swinging level boils down to directing all the force of your bat straight ahead through the ball. For a pitch at the belt, this means you're always swinging trying to crush a three-foot high line drive to the fence. This is called "driving the ball" and all great hitters try to do it. The smart ones listen.

Coaching Tip: "Feel the "Force" (Blind)

Just swing your bat, no frills. The secret is to close your eyes and actually feel the force and path your swing. Is it being directed down and straight out, swish — or are you unconsciously lifting? Are you actually swinging for a three foot high rope? Make sure you are, and do it many times to build the habit.

Coaching Tip: Did You Know?

Grounders are 15% more likely to produce base hits than fly balls.

Inside Gimmick: "Unforgettable"

Realize how the correct swing is like a "swish" and the dreaded uppercut is like a "happy face" smile. These useful images are hard to forget.

Never Try to Lift the Ball

Good hitters never attempt to lift the ball, or uppercut. They just hit down through it and try to drive it hard straight ahead. You must continually strive for line drives to hit your best. What follows should convince you.

Master Coaching Tip: "Eat, Sleep, and Dream Line Drives"

Always view your batting practice as line drive practice instead. Coaches, you too, including assistants. Keep repeating, "line drives or hard grounders" until your players are sick of it. They'll end up thanking you later.

Missing Under Phenomenon: Top Half Remedy

Hitters usually miss by swinging under the ball, particularly on any fastballs. Need some common sense proof. Ask yourself this: How many balls do you see the pros foul off downward compared to upward?

Whenever you are missing, try to hit the "top half of the ball." Percentages show if you don't miss under, you'll hardly miss. Get in the habit of beginning batting practice by starting out hitting "top half" grounders and then gradually work up to line shots. This will help you get started making contact quicker. It also helps train you to swing under less and not to uppercut. Remember, if you're struggling with your contact try to "get on top" and hit the top half of the ball. That way you're more likely to "find the ball."

It's hard to overrate the importance of this phenomenon to a hitter. There is nothing that wrecks a batter's confidence more than not being able to make contact. This confidence is pretty much everything. Once a hitter actually learns that he's most certainly missing just under fastballs, his confidence can soar. By now, knowing to "get on top a little" his performance can skyrocket.

Many times in lessons, I purposely tell "whiffing" batters to try to actually miss the ball by swinging barely over it.

It's amazing, the looks on their faces, when they start to hit and keep making really solid contact. It sounds funny: By trying to miss, they start to hit. It just confirms the value of getting on top.

Coaching Tip: "Top Half Pays Off"

Now that you know this stuff, make use of it. You can use a "top half" or "get on top of the ball" strategy to minimize missing with two-strike counts, or when you want a ground ball to score or advance a runner.

Master Coaching Tip: "Whiffing Fix"

Most batters miss for only two reasons: Being late and swinging under. If you're "whiffing," try to "hit the top half" of the ball and hit it "out in front" on time. Batters who are "on time" and "on top" hardly miss.

How To Miss-Hit the Ball Better

Statistics prove most of the balls you hit, will be miss-hit — not on the sweet spot of the bat or the middle of the ball. By continually practicing line drives, the most perfect contact, your miss-hits will be much more accurate than otherwise.

You'll hit more home runs by trying to hit line drives. In fact, you'll hit more of everything, because you'll make more and better contact, and strike out less. Take a moment to really let that sink in. Coaches should faithfully remind hitters, "line drives or hard grounders" in practice and games.

Coaching Tip: "Uppercutting?"

Players should expect to hit at least one third of their hits on the ground. If you don't, it's likely you have at least a moderate uppercut.

Coaching Tip: "Think of It as an "Undercut"

One kid said "undercut" instead of uppercut. Think of it as undercutting, and it's clearer how you avoid it. With a proper chop swing, staying on top of the ball longer.

Level Swing Drills

1. The "swish" drill: The player puts a mark on any wall, even with his belt buckle. Draw, or use tape, a straight five-foot-long line centered on this mark. Have the line drop eight inches over its length. Four inches on each side of the mark (see drawing Fig. 6.3). Stand centered on the line, and just try to make your hands follow the line as you swing. Follow through normally. You're practicing the "swish" shape of the perfect chop swing.

2. Level swing tee work: Don't neglect this one. Hit off a "tee." Try to hit pure line drives over and over until you can regularly hit seven

out of ten. You must swing level to do this. Line drives are always proof of a level swing. Set up for inside and outside pitch locations and work on your line drive percentage for those as well.

Mechanical Tips: "Level Rotation"

When you swing, your hips should stay level, no matter how low the pitch. Don't squat or sit down as you hit. Simply chop your hands down more as necessary (see Fig. 6.4). Never lower your legs to the ball, just your hands. That way your head can remain still.

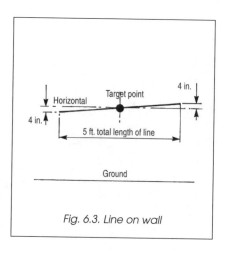

Fig. 6.3. Line on wall

Coaching Tip: "Watch the Hitching"

Some batters set up correctly but drop their hands with a hitch. This can actually force you to uppercut. If you end up hitching your hands down very far, they can end up below some high strikes. To hit these pitches, you then have to swing uphill.

Finishing Long Through the Ball

One key to a level swing is full extension whenever possible, finishing long. You want to hit right through the ball, not to it. This encourages drives. Always extend your bat head straight on through every ball until you can't extend more.

Finishing Long Drills

Work on a tee. Have a helper hold up two additional balls in front of one on it. Then take a swing, after the extra balls are removed, that would slice through all three (see Fig. 6.6). In batting practice, swing as if you are hitting through three balls. Think of "cutting the ball in half." That action involves swinging all the way through.

Fig. 6.5. Player chops his hands down to a low ball but his hips turn and stay level.

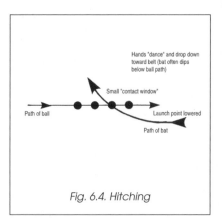

Hands "dance" and drop down toward belt (bat often dips below ball path)

Small "contact window"

Path of ball

Launch point lowered

Path of bat

Fig. 6.4. Hitching

Uppercutting

The opposite of an ideal level downswing is called an uppercut, the dreaded uphill swing. It rates its own section because there is no defect more common or devastating to your performance than uppercutting. The dipping path of an uppercut drops your bat head below the path and plane of the ball. This means your timing must be almost perfect to bring your bat head back up at just the right time to make contact (see Fig. 6.2). To put it another way, if your timing isn't so good, you'll miss. If you're late you'll almost always get "caught" somewhere under the ball. That means you'll either mis, or miss-hit at best. It's a high trib-ute to the amazing abilities of some human beings that uppercutters hit anything at all.

Uppercutting just makes all kinds of bad things more likely. Strike-outs, foul ball strikes, pop ups, fly-outs, and ironically weak topped grounders. What it doesn't do is produce many line drives and hard ground balls. Those happen to be the hits that get you on base best and produce the most runs to help your team win. In spite of all this, it's clear that human beings still love to uppercut, trying to hit high long deep home runs and fly balls.

There are two giant misconceptions here. First is that high-fly balls are desirable. However spectacular, high fly balls end up being outs way

Fig. 6.6. Swinging as if you are trying to hit through three balls encourages drives.

more often than plain hard grounders. For every long high-fly ball that manages to find a gap, four or five are caught for outs. The more advanced the level, the more this is true.

The second problem is that many hitters truly believe they have to swing uphill to hit the ball a long way in the air. A dead level or slightly downhill stroke actually produces more deep drives by increasing both solid contact and backspin for carry.

Uppercutting is for suckers. That's why the third set rule of my hitting system is, "no uphill swings."

How to Identify an Uppercut

The simplest way is to carefully study the path of the batter's hands and bat head during the swing for a good while. Pay special attention to the track through the contact zone. This is pretty much from the batter's front hip, and then out a foot. If the hitter's swing path is consistently headed uphill in this contact area, you can be sure he's uppercutting.

Hint:

On low pitches it's harder to tell, because there's always somewhat of a down-and-up profile to those swings. It'll be much easier to recognize on a belt high and up-pitch.

Tip:

Guys with high golf-like finishes are much more likely to be uppercutters. You won't see nearly as many with players who have lower, flatter follow-throughs.

Once you suspect uppercutting, you can further confirm it by evaluating these: Look at the front arm and elbow during the swing. Think of these as kind of like a bird's wing. If this "wing" points uphill anytime approaching impact during the swing, that indicates an uppercut. Uppercutters' swings are almost always curvy looking, like the curvy smile you see on those yellow happy faces. Guys who swing level tend to have swings that look downhill longer, and much straighter. A "swish" shape rather than a smile.

It used to really bug me, because some of my son's coaches were telling him he was uppercutting, only because they could see his back shoulder was dropping. This is not a reliable way to identify an uppercut. On any good pitch, low enough you'd want to swing at it, the rear shoulder will correctly and naturally drop below the front one. In fact, the physical anatomy of the human being compels it. This is simply because your shoulders are physically located well above any good swingable pitches down in the zone. So depend on the swing and hand paths and the front elbow assessment to sniff out uppercuts, not the shoulder positions.

Uppercut Breaker Drill/Level Swing Maker: "Tee-and-Stick Drill"

The significance of this drill is nothing short of earthshaking. Uppercutting is a swing killer, and this can absolutely cure it. You just have to do enough repetitions. Set up a batting "tee," mid-thigh high. Pound a stick or thin rod, (for example, half-inch EMT or rebar) into the ground, one half inch below the tee top (see Fig. 6.7). Now just start hitting balls off the tee without letting your bat hit the pole. Commit yourself to try to hit the very middle of each ball. Resist any temptation to cheat by aiming higher. There is an important additional lesson to be learned here: You will see complete proof how it's possible to hit line shots well up in the air with a swing that's actually slightly downhill.

This drill is failproof. You must swing level or you will hit the stick. Work until you can constantly line the ball without any stick contact. If you have two "tees" you can overlap the rear one to get the same set up.

Note:

Use an old bat for this drill because naturally it can get scratched. Once you're proficient at pocket-high balls, try other settings.

Coaching Tip: "Flaps Down"

You never want your front elbow up nearing contact. Work on this when you warm up and in practice. Think of your bent front arm as a wing flap. Now

Above: Fig. 6.7. This set-up can be used to eliminate uppercutting.

Below: Fig. 6.8. Tipping your shoulders uphill can easily lead to an uppercut.

be sure your "wing" stays somewhat down as you attack the ball, never up (see "core section" photos on pages 56 through 58). Up means an uppercut.

"Set-Up Nightmare"

This really isn't a drill per se, but just a heads up to be aware of a set-up flaw that can induce uppercutting. For reasons unknown, some batters will set up with their shoulders tilted uphill (see Fig. 6.8). This incorrect set-up can easily lead to an uppercut. With your torso already pointed uphill, the hands are likely to follow that lead.

Batters should start their set-ups by standing naturally, like standing around talking with friends. That should take care of this. No one I know stands casually with their shoulders tipped uphill. It doesn't hurt for you to imagine two full glasses of water sitting on your shoulders. Then you can just think about standing with your shoulders level, so that no water would spill from either glass.

7.

Master Secret No. 3:
The Secrets of Timing

Another secret to hitting is to consistently hit the ball somewhere "in front" of your body (see Fig. 7.1). That's where you see it best (see "Out in Front," page 42), and where the most power and bat speed is achieved.

The "I" in the "WIN" System: "In Front" Contact

When your "out in front" timing is perfect, it's called the "hammer" or power position. The timing of great hitters is always right around the hammer. "Out in front timing" and the "hammer" are habits. They require work. They must be developed by specifically targeting them in practice.

Out in Front Batting Practice

Hitting the ball "out in front" is not natural. Set aside part of your batting practice to work solely on this timing. First, work on making contact somewhere out in front of your eyes and hip over and over. Try to be on time every swing, but never late.

Once you dial in your "habit" of constant out in front contact, you can move on to trying for the perfect hammer power positions.

Learning the Hammer and Hammer Rehearsal

Use a special pre-swing routine. Figures 7.2 through 7.7 show two views of the hammer positions for outside, middle, and inside pitches. You will be practicing the middle hammer. Ever seen Mike Piazza at bat? He takes slow half swings, rehearsing a perfect "cut," stopping right at the middle power posi-tion. He even practices turning his head down to watch impact.

You will use the same routine, only in batting practice. Take a couple of slow precise half swings ending in the perfect power position. On the last one, clearly imagine hitting the upcoming pitch in that exact power position (see Figs. 7.4 and 7.5) Then try to crush the next pitch dead on in your hammer. Have a coach "spot" and tell you how perfect, late, or early your actual timing and power position was for that pitch location.

Figs. 7.1. This batter is striking the ball well out in front of his eyes, where he can see it best.

From left to right and from top to bottom: Figs. 7.2, 7.3 (top row), Figs. 7.4, 7.5 (middle row), Figs. 7.6, 7.7 (bottom row). Progressive steps in the swing sequence for the hammer routine. The photos on the left show a frontal view, those on the right a top view.

Above: Fig. 7.8. Outside hammer off tee.

Below: Fig. 7.9, Middle hammer off tee.

Coaching Tip: "Don't Be Dumb"

Some batters take rehearsal half swings between pitches in actual games. That make no sense. You'll often see pre swing rituals that are more suitable for practicing a chip shot than hitting a baseball. How stupid is this? You need to take every opportunity to rehearse and reinforce a correct swing pathway like you're going to use. Not some golf swing. Equally dense is to warm up in

Fig. 7.10. Inside hammer off tee.

the on deck circle, or anywhere else, taking swings as if pitches were at your shoulders or down by your feet. Think about it: Both these practices eventually result in thousands of repetitions training muscle memories that are wrong. Hitting is hard enough. Practicing mistakes is beyond dumb.

Above: Fig. 7.11. Hold racket in the middle hammer vertically, and then grip it flat-handed.
Below: Fig. 7.12. Draw back the racket.

Fig. When you hit a sharp liner, you have achieved a flat-handed hammer.

Coaching Tip: "Golden Timing"

The "golden rules" for good batting practice timing are better early than late, and on top rather than under. These will counteract the powerful tendencies to be late and swing under that hurt most hitters.

Hammer Tee Drill — Ideal Positions for Various Pitches

Set up a tee and pose in each "hammer" before hitting, for inside, middle, and outside pitches (see Figs. 7.8 through

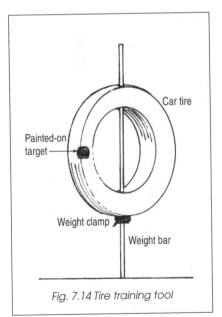

Fig. 7.14 Tire training tool

7.10). Notice how ideal power positioning hits the ball where it is pitched. Inside to left, middle in between left and right center, and outside toward right. This will help you learn to "go with the pitch," for the most effective hitting.

"Hammer" Training Tools: The Tire

Babe Ruth chopped trees to train. That way he could feel, and actually see, just how much power he was delivering right at impact. Don't chop down any trees just yet. Build a device per drawing Fig. 7.14 instead. Get an old weight bar with one sliding collar and an old tire. Hit the tire, and it will spin roughly in proportion to how hard and solid your blow. It's how much bat speed you can muster by impact that counts. This device will teach you to maximize your velocity right at impact rather than later, where it's wasted.

Tennis Racket Trainer — "Flat-Handed" Hammer

When you swing an ax, the shape of its handle holds your hands in a "flat-handed" position. The fact that your palms face each other is on purpose. This is the strongest position for your hands. It efficiently concentrates all your power to the center of an ax blade — or a baseball bat. Ideally, you always want your hands in this perfect "flat hand" position at impact. A flat handed hammer is the ultimate goal for hitters.

Here's how to practice it. Use any tennis racket (you can get them cheap at thrift stores or garage sales) and practice hitting tennis or wiffle balls as if it was a bat. Before starting, hold your racket in the hammer rehearsal position, racket face perpendicular. Be sure to grip it flat-handed (see Fig. 7.11). Keeping this grip, assume your batting stance (see Fig. 7.12). Now, just swing away trying to hit "ropes," line drives. You will be practicing the ideal flat-handed position each time you succeed in producing a line shot (see Fig. 7.13).

8.

The Secrets of Power

At one of my kids' games, I was shooting the breeze with a high school batting coach. We were talking about various hitters on the team. He made this comment about a kid that had caught my eye: "Yeah he's got lots of power, lots of bat speed, you just can't teach that."

I remember thinking, are my ears plugged? Did I really just hear that? Fortunately, for you hitters reading this book, this is complete nonsense. If you can't teach power, you can't teach anything. Power is a combination of the right mechanics and habits. Any hitter can learn and improve power habits and mechanics. I promise you.

Bat Head Speed — "Throwing the Bat Head" and "Quick Twitch"

The swing is really a "throw." Practice "throwing the bat head." It's bat head speed that really matters. Key on quickness, not raw power. Try for an explosive hip turn and snappy chain reaction that fires your hands and whips your bat head harder and harder. It should feel like you're actually trying to "throw" and accelerate the barrel lightning fast at the ball. A lot like you were trying to fling a powerful refrigerator magnet off the end of a steel bat.

Coaching Tip: "Knot Bad"

Make a "throwing" trainer: Get a scrap of hose and tie a big knot on one end (see Fig. 8.1). You just throw the knot lightning fast at any fence, with the proper chop swing. That's exactly how it feels to really

Fig. 8.1. Throwing the bat head should feel a lot like throwing this knotted hose.

"fling" the bat head. While it's fresh in your mind, get a bat and duplicate that explosive throw, swinging it. Don't actually throw the bat.

Quick Twitch

"Quick twitch" builds quickness. Swing a very light bat or a "speed stick" (see page 102) really fast, daily. Over time, the muscles memorize this quicker firing which "revs up" your swing. Those thin plastic toy bats and wiffle golf balls work great.

Master Coaching Tip: "The Trick is Quick"

Work obsessively on increasing the quickness of your swing from launch to impact. Each fraction of a second you shave off means you can wait until the ball is several feet closer before swinging. This is gigantic. A scant twentieth of a second with a sixty-five-mph pitch, for example, means you get almost five feet longer to more accurately gauge exactly where the ball is, and whether there's any break. Greatness comes in tiny fractions of a second.

Where's the Beef?

What part of your body supplies almost all the power of your swing?

Kneel down, with you knees and ankles touching, and swing the bat hard (see Fig. 8.2). Now stand up and swing hard again. By purposely taking away all your leg and hip power, it now becomes obvious that the hips and legs supply the real power.

Here's how that occurs. The key is a fast, full, and powerful rotation of the hips (see Fig. 8.3). It is this explosive "turning on the ball" that produces the extreme power and quickness you need. This is called rotational hitting. The next section will show you how to get the most out of this hip and leg drive.

Learning an Explosive Turn "Spotlight Drill"

Imagine you have three miniature spotlights, one on each

Above: Fig. 8.2. Do this and you'll be certain where the power comes from. Below: Fig. 8.3. A correct weight shift stays inside your legs, hence the front leg often stiffens.

Figs. 8.4 (above) and 8.5 (below). Placing a bat behind your back will cause your body to work in unison.

knee and your belt buckle. Now take powerful swings where the back foot pivots, like mashing a bug, and the hips turn fully so that all three beams would hit the pitcher every time (see Fig. 4.11 on page 46).

The Mechanics of the Weight Shift

Try to always begin doing the "spotlight drill" with a bat behind your back (see Figs. 8.4 and 8.5). The purpose of this is to cause your entire body to turn together and work as a unit.

The ideal of getting your entire body to work together is terribly important. If you cock the bat in "one piece," and launch in unison, your entire mass starts and drives the bat. This lets you "overpower" it. The bat behind the back gets your body segments working nicely together. Golfers have known this for years.

Now hold your bat as usual in the correct set-up. Practice the perfect rotational weight shift and swing. It's important to understand that there are actually two turns in rotational hitting.

The first is a small backward turn that simultaneously loads your power and the bat back. During this turn, shift your weight back and begin loading it strongly against the inside of your back leg and foot. Then, as you stride, load your weight back even more by continuing your backward turn and coil a little more.

Now fully loaded, launch your swing and shift by simultaneously turning hard with your hips and pivoting strongly on your back foot. This is called turning on the ball, and this is how you can generate the most power very quickly. If you turn on the ball right, it feels like all your weight is being shifted, spun, and then slammed against the inside of your braced front leg. One characteristic of rotational hitters is a stiff front leg on most pitches. This is the opposite of a long weight slide and shift. With proper rotation it always feels like you're hitting with your weight behind and against your front leg, never lunging out over it. A rotational weight shift stays between the insides of your legs (see Fig. 8.3).

This is what spins your weight and then catapults tremendous leg energy into your upper body (see Fig. 7.6 on page 74). This is an incredibly explosive and powerful spin, brake, and fling action similar to an Olympian throwing a discuss. Your hip rotation is the rocket motor that launches, drives, and whips the bat.

Starting your rotation practice with a bat behind your back virtually makes you do the mechanics correctly. Take plenty of time to figure it out and get it right.

Once you get a coordinated feel for weight shifting with the bat behind your back, remove it. Then continue to practice the spotlight drill swinging your bat normally. Be sure to start slow, find proper form, and then gradually work up to lightning quick power turns. Always check for the essential strong back foot pivot, like mashing a bug, and a complete full turn of all your "spots." It really helps to regularly hold up in your full follow-through position. By freezing your swing at this point, you can

now carefully look down to verify if both knees got completely around and your back foot pivoted up fully.

About 70 percent of your power comes from this hip drive. This hip pivot is the heart and soul of your power. Practice it hard.

Coaching Tip: "Batless in Seattle — or Elsewhere"

Try practicing the spotlight drill without a bat. Just clasp your hands together (see Figs. 8.6 and 8.7). Minus the bat, you can now focus even more closely on the pure mechanics and muscle memories of a blazing hip pivot. Hands-only drills are truly beautiful. They can be done about anywhere at any time. Even better, they virtually eliminate any excuses for not practicing based on not having any equipment or time to get to a field. I often suggest students do these every commercial when they're watching television.

Figs. 8.6 (above) and 8.7 (below). Hands-only swings can intensify your sense of the pure mechanics of the swing.

Coaching Tip: "A Word of Caution"

There's a pitfall to watch out for even if you are a rotational hitter: turning fully. Never just spin with all the weight on your back foot without any forward shift. It will be relatively compact, but there is a definite weight shift from the inside of your back leg to the inside of your front leg. Shifting is vital to any swing.

Rotational Hitting Versus Weight Sliding

The whole purpose of the spotlight drill and the bat behind your back is to teach you how to hit by "turning on the ball." Your most explosive swing is achieved by rotating your weight and power back and forth. Many batters want to shift their weight inefficiently, by sliding it ahead in a more lunging style with insufficient hip turn. Be advised that nearly all young kids tend to swing this way. This is one of the biggest reasons why so many young hitters always tend to be late.

If you're a player who gets a lot of stingers from hitting balls near your hands, take a good look at this one as the culprit. To hit any fast inside pitch, you must be able to rotate your hands quickly and pull them in fast around in front of your body, to get the fat part of the bat in on the ball (see Figs. 7.6 and 7.7 on page 74). That's pretty hard to do if your bat is sliding linear style. What we're really talking about here is the difference between dragging the bat to the ball versus turning and throwing it at the ball. These are two distinct styles of hitting. It's obvious which one I, and every other power hitter on the planet, favors.

Harnessing Power — "Leading With the Knob"

There is a secret to harnessing all your energy and translating it all into bat head speed. You need to lead your swing with the knob of the bat (see Fig. 8.7 and "core section" photos on pages 56–58). When you launch your swing it should feel a lot like you're attacking the ball

with the "knob," firing it at the target. This keeps your bat head back, delaying its release. This "whips" the bat head, causing rapid acceleration when it is forced to catch up with your hands near impact. Only by leading with the knob, inside the ball's path, and whipping the bat head, will you get all possible bat head speed. Here's a drill to teach you how:

Above: Fig. 8.8. Setting distance parallel to the barrier.
Below: Fig. 8.9. Leading with the knob and staying close. Note the bent front arm

Fig. 8.10. Follow through normally after your bat clears the barrier.

The Barrier Drill

Stand squarely facing a wall or fence. Hold your bat straight out, so it touches the barrier and your belt buckle. This sets your distance. Now take strong level swings, belt-high, without letting the end of the bat touch the barrier (see Figs. 8.8 through 8.10).

Early in the swing, this forces you to drastically lead with the knob, keeping your hands in tight, and the bat head well back. Once your hands eventually clear the wall, follow through normally. Hint: Take some slow motion swings to figure out what has to happen for this to work. Then, speed up slowly.

This drill should win an award. It works even if you don't understand it. It trains the perfect late release anyway.

It forces any batters with long sweeping strokes into an efficient compact swing. It trains the inside-out stroke, starting close, and keeping your hands inside the ball.

During this drill, tune into the power of the snap, roll-over, of your wrists as they whip so fast late in the swing. That powerful, explosive snap signals you're getting the hyper bat speed the drill teaches.

Coaching Tips: "Throw the Knob Drill" and "Imaginary Barrier Drill"

Do some barrier drill just before your turn in batting practice. When you get up, try to hit by "firing the knob at the ball." Attack with the knob.

Also try some "imaginary barrier" drill. Right at the plate, in between pitches. Just "picture" as solid wall right in front of you. Even hold your bat out from your belt buckle as usual. The wall will be only imaginary, but the results will be real enough.

Coaching Tip: "Habits Aren't Accidental"

Power is a habit. Bat speed is a habit. These you have to earn by hard, inspired work on a tee and soft toss. The key is to always practice swinging explosively, right up to the point where you lose a little balance. That'll guarantee you'll always push your speed and power limits.

"Sweeping is for Brooms"

"Sweeping" occurs when you launch your swing with a front arm that is too straight, often locked at the elbow as in golf. An overly stiff arm causes a long, slow, sweeping swing arc. It also throws away all the potential power from properly un-coiling your arm and wrist. It makes you drag your bat.

Sweeping is for brooms, not for bats. Here's what to watch out for. Some batters set up with their arm too straight. Some straighten it out too much as they . The worst is when batters start their swing with a downward hitch, locking the arm and uncocking the wrist, called "locking and sweeping" (see Fig. 8.11). Lots of barrier drills will help cure these.

Fig. 8.11. A sweeper with a "long," straight arm.

Coiling and Wrapping: Extra Power

You've heard the expression "loaded for bear." Batters should load maximum power too, both in the stance and when they coil back to "cock" the swing.

the wrist, the small backward turns of the hip, shoulder, and knee, all load power. The more you coil, the more power you store for release. Like pulling back a spring. Watch Ken Griffey's powerful coil for example.

The only correct limitations for coiling are the following:

- ❏ You must keep both eyes on the ball.

- ❏ You must "stay tall," without leaning or crouching.

- ❏ You will need to turn, not lean, your body as a unit and never coil so much that your back eye gets pulled off the ball.

Check three body points to verify complete coiling. the front shoulder, hip, and knee (see Fig. 8.12).

Avoid hitching when you coil. When you your swing, you need to take your hands almost straight back. Don't dance them up and down as you coil. This useless movement wrecks consistency, no matter how good it often feels.

Above: Fig. 8.12. Coiling fully stores tremendous energy for release.

Below: Fig. 8.13. Body coiling will cock your bat without hitching.

Hitch Breaker

End hitching your hands by body coiling them back. During your loading, act like your body and hands are locked together. Now turn back your front hip and knee by rotating back your front hip inward a little so it faces the pitcher slightly (see Fig. 8.11). Your

whole body will then coil as a unit, taking your hands almost straight back. "Groove" body coiling your hands. Tell yourself, "straight back, straight to the ball."

Here's a neat gimmick to help you learn quicker. At set up, tuck a D-cell battery under your front arm pit so it barely stays. Now swing. If it doesn't fall out in the coiling phase of your swing, you're doing it perfectly.

"Wrapping" the Bat

During the load, cocking your wrists so the bat head ends up pointing forward is called "wrapping" (see Fig. 8.12). It is surprisingly controversial. What's important, if you don't cock your wrists, you loose power. Your hands travel the same distance in the same time anyway, whether the wrists are cocked or not. With cocked wrists your bat head will travel several inches further in virtually the same time.

This means more bat speed for free. Get a clue. Most pros and good little leaguers do it. Don't be confused. Never wrap by moving your hands more around behind your head. Just wrap the bat head itself by simply cocking your wrists. Wrapping your bat head this right way generates tremendous power.

Here's an explanation of how to wrap efficiently: Take a good look at the correct starting position for the bat head in the "core section" photographs on pages 56 through 58. The first thing to notice is that, though the bat head does start out wrapped, it's on the modest side. You want the full wrapping and of the bat to happen later as a smooth integral part of the load. A simple slight cocking of your wrist as your hands draw back is what you're after. Do this, and you create an exquisitely effective trigger movement that all at once breaks inertia, starts your bat, and sets up tremendous whip and bat speed.

Here's the only tricky part: Some batters set up wrapped too much or too little to begin with. If you're too wrapped, you inhibit the dynamic starting movement you need. If you're not wrapped enough, you'll have excessive movement that lessens control. The key is to study and copy the pictures closely so you'll reap the tremendous benefits of wrapping correctly.

For maximum power, start in a strong position, and then fully coil to your strongest possible position. The idea is to load every speck of energy for crushing the ball. If you're going hunting, why not get "loaded for bear"?

Coaching Tip: "Using Your Head"

When you keep your head down on contact you get much more power from the muscles of the top of your shoulders and neck into the ball.

9.

The Stride

The stride actually starts your swing before the pitch is released. This makes your bat "lighter" and quicker, buying you extra time to react. It gives you a "head start" on the ball. This inertia-busting movement is crucial for hitting fast pitching.

Stride Mechanics — Overstriding

The most efficient stride is short, about three or four inches, and lands just before the pitch is released. A short stride cuts down your forward head and eye movement. It's quicker, so you can wait and see the ball longer. For off-speed pitches, this is huge. With a short stride, you not only get a longer look at the break, but it's easier to keep your weight back and adjust.

Too big a stride is called overstriding. It slows your swing, requiring you to step very early. This can cause you to get your weight out on your front foot too early, which dissipates all your power. That's how overstriding often makes you "a sitting duck" for change-of-speed pitches.

Coaching Tip: "Curing Early Release"

Even with a short stride, you can fall into the habit of releasing forward too soon. Batters just step or uncoil too early. If you often swing but seem to have to hold up and then restart, that's a tip-off.

Correct this in batting practice. The simplest method is to hit balls to your opposite field for a while. This automatically makes you "stay back" and wait better. An alternate cure is to try keeping your front shoulder pointing at each pitch until you feel you can't wait any longer before swinging. Keeping this shoulder "in" helps keep you from opening up, uncoiling, too early. Try out both techniques. They also help with outright lunging.

Coiling, Cocking, and Your Stride

You need to coil when you stride. It's essential to cock back your shoulders, hands, and hips to keep your power back, even as you step and start forward. Good hitters actually load more and more weight back on their rear foot as they step forward. This is the only way to hit offspeed well. In a nutshell, here's what you're after, every time. Whenever your stride goes forward, your hands and weight go backward. That's why it's called separating (see below).

Coaching Tip: "Detailed Explanation for Coaches"

A correct swing starts with a slow pre-coil before the step, driving weight back against your rear foot. As your stride foot leaves the ground, you quickly cock back a little more. This instantly locks almost all your energy to the rear foot and leg for launch, because you stand on the back leg for an instant. That's why an explosive rear foot pivot is so vital. The actual inertia breaking is done by the forward momentum of the step, and a subtle lowering of the center of gravity, because when you step you drop slightly. Coiling and wrapping puts the bat in motion. This makes it much "lighter" and quicker than if it were stopped dead.

Coil, Separate, and Launch

So much for explanations. It's fairly easy to learn all these complicated sounding mechanics.

Note:

You can't think about doing these in actual games. You must practice until they become automatic. Here's how:

Figs. 9.1 (above) and 9.2 (below). The bungee drill makes it easier to learn how to separate.

Think of your swing as three parts to practice in rapid sequence: coil, separate, and launch. Begin coiling slowly; then stride forward while still coiling back, as if trying to separate your hands and striding foot away from each other; then launch. This can be beautifully taught in a big group with everyone lined up and a coach calling out, "coil, separate, and launch." Separating is big. This is how you "keep your power back" and start forward at the same time.

Master Coaching Tip: "Stretch the Bungee Drill"

Here's a trick to make this simple. You can either do it or just imagine it. Imagine a long bungee cord attached to your front foot and your hands. The idea is to coil back as you stride forward, stretching out the bungee cord, by separating, in the process (see Figs. 9.1 and 9.2). If you just imagine stretching the cord, or actually do it, you can't help but get the right idea. Now it's coil, stretch the cord, launch.

Important: at high levels, coiling is shorter, quick, and subtle. It's harder to see and feel. Be sure you're still separating, even if it is short and quick.

"Dead Hands"

If your hands don't move backward before the swing, you are a "dead " who isn't separating. Imagine this: You're at a carnival that has one of those amusements where you hit a punching bag your hardest, and it says whether you're Mike Tyson or a wuss. You have one punch to impress your friends. Go ahead and throw that punch. Now why did you cock your hand way back before you punched? That's right: "to get more power." It makes you think, doesn't it? Imagine the same amusement only rigged up stronger so you can use a bat. Now, take the same blow knowing everybody's watching, only with a bat. Get it? You need to coil back and "load" up to hit a baseball your hardest too. Pitchers "wind up" for power. Hitters need to "wind up" for power by cocking their swing and hands back.

Master Coaching Tip: "Load Your Gun"

This helps: I tell students, "you have to load your gun, before you can fire your gun. I have them say when they coil, "load the gun," and as they launch, " fire the gun."

Important: If you're constantly late, rule out dead hands first. It's likely the culprit. A "dead" bat is a slow bat.

Coaching Tip: "Dead Hands CPR"

You can practice eliminating dead hands with soft toss. You just make sure you cock your hands back each time the tosser's hand goes back to deliver the ball. It's that simple.

Timing Out the Coiling/Stride

The secret to timing out the coiling is this well worn advice: "When the pitcher winds up by showing you his hip, you wind up by coiling yours." Do this by slightly rotating back your hip, striding, and cocking your knee. This makes your stride foot land slightly closed (see Fig. 8.12 and 8.13 on page 89). This body coil "cocks" everything properly: hip, shoulder, hands, and knees.

Players should try this out in batting practice and in the group "coil separate" drill described before. The coach can simulate pitching. This will get you close to the right timing and you can refine it from there.

Step Every Pitch

All good hitters step every pitch, whether they swing or not. If you've worked hard on the previous material, you'll be able to do this and keep your hands and weight back, and ready. Coaches should pull surprise checks by stopping their deliveries abruptly and see if everyone stepped anyway. This works very well in soft toss. Be sure you are starting every pitch. To be a good hitter, you have to plan on swinging at every pitch right up until you don't. It is the proper coiling, and separating that allows you this luxury.

Master Coaching Tip: "Easy Does It"

You want a low, soft stride that lands like you were stepping on eggshells you didn't want to break. This softness helps you hang your weight back, even while stepping forward. "A soft step equals a powerful bat."

Coaching Tip: "Tippy Toeing" for Power?

A correct stride is not only soft it should land toe first and slightly closed (see Fig. 9.4). "tippy toeing" your stride's landing helps even more to insure you'll "stay back" properly. It's hard to put a lot of weight on "tippy toes." This time it's "macho" to tippy toe.

Coaching Tip: "Lose the One-Legger"

Some players take a big, high leg coil, like a pitcher's leg kick.

Don't do this. You are striding with one leg high in the air and balancing on the other one until the right time (see Fig. 9.3). These circus acrobatics are much harder to perform and time than a short, low, and soft step.

Eliminating Overstriding, "Stepping in the Bucket," etc.

The "No-Stride"

This is a great example of overcorrecting to retrain. It is the very best cure for

Below: Fig. 9.3. Tippy-toeing your stride landing helps keep your weight back.

Right: Fig. 9.4. Avoid this kind of "one-leg acrobatics."

overstriding, stepping out, etc. The idea is to go to no-striding for as long as it takes to reeducate the body. You can learn a perfect textbook stride with this process. The no stride even teaches weight slide hitters to turn on the ball (see page 81, "Weight Shift").

It is often the only way to get pronounced weight sliders hitters to quickly execute and experience what turning on the ball is about. A perfect stride is three or four inches and should angle in toward the plate at about 30 degrees. It should be landed toe first with the foot a little closed, toe in slightly to keep power back. Anytime you your swing with the correct one-piece turn, the backward hip rotation and resulting knee cock closes your foot a little automatically.

To "no-stride," the hitter steps out and pre-sets up in this perfect stride landing position to begin with (see Figs. 9.4 and 9.5). Then to swing, the batter just slams his front heel down and squishes the bug simultaneously, making sure not to step (see Fig. 9.6).

Above: Fig. 9.5. No-stride set-up position.
Below: To swing, you just slam down your front heel and pivot your back foot simultaneously.

Note:

Be sure you your knee and raise your front heel as pictured (see Fig. 9.5). The uncocking and planting/pivoting movement of your knee and foot, take the place of a stride, and keeps your weight back.

It's important you understand that the end goal is not a permanent swing with no stride at all. The no-stride is only a necessary means to an end. The end goal is a very short but definite stride of only about three inches. With this in mind, you'll want to monitor progress very closely. Periodically swing normally without pre-striding or thinking. once you see a consistent short three-inch stride, you can stop. If crops up again, just resume the drill until it's under control.

Coaching Tip: "Two Wrongs Don't…"

The popular notion of fixing stepping out with a very open stance to force closing up properly is nuts (see Fig. 9.7). These band-aid solutions just substitute one defect for another. Use the pre-stride instead. That way everything starts and stays correct without requiring any disruptive movement.

The Latest: the "Back-Step"

This book is committed to bringing you worthwhile innovations. The "back-step" is a new stride technique rapidly gaining popularity.

A big part of its appeal is how easy it is to learn. You start

Fig. 9.7. Do not use a defective stance to correct another problem.

out in a pre-strided position, placing your front foot out in the perfect stride landing position to start with. As the pitcher brings his hand back, or shows his hip, you bring your front foot backward into the normal narrower set up position, with a three or four inch back-step. At this time, you load your weight back. To swing, you just step forward and replant, returning your front foot to the perfect stride landing position you just started in. It's as simple as retracing your step.

For most people, this is easier to learn than coil, separate, and launch. Perhaps most people don't know the bungee gimmick. The only drawbacks are that the back-step adds an extra step, literally. Also, the back-and-forward step sequence slightly creates a tendency to weight-slide a little longer before turning. The main thing is it works.

Try mastering coil, separate, and launch first. If you really can't get it, then try the back-step. This is the first good alternative ever and is really easy to learn. Because you retrace and replace your step in the correct landing position, it also works well to prevent stepping out.

10.

The Best Ways to Train Your Hitting

The golden rule for all training — there is only one way to ever train: Do it right! Don't ever settle for practicing your old "comfy" swing, with all its comfy flaws. Practice correctly, no matter what, even if it doesn't work or feel good right away.

Truly, "Practice doesn't make perfect. Perfect practice makes perfect." Make sure you understand the difference.

I'm constantly pleading with my students, "Don't worry about the results. Worry about the quality of your swing." You must develop the correct habits to hit your best. Habits that can be attained only

Figs. 10.1. Some really simple and inexpensive but effective training aids.

by lots of quality repetitions, doing only the right stuff, over and over. No substitutes, no shortcuts.

Unfortunately, many of the most important hitting drills that follow are not what you would call exciting or glamorous. The good news is that few people will have the discipline or drive to put in the necessary hard work. Those who do will excel and stand out even more.

Physical Strength Training

The temptation is to get really complicated and high-tech, but you don't need to. I almost hate to disappoint all the would-be personal trainers out there. Three old-fashioned favorites will get you all the results you need, without need of any fancy equipment or facilities. This eliminates all the excuses and travel time.

❏ Push ups: builds the triceps muscle strength to drive and throw your hands powerfully.

❏ Sit ups: strengthening the pelvic girdle can do the most for your hitting All that critical rotational power from your torso depends on strong stomach muscles and structures.

❏ Wrist rollers: see "Give Them a Hand" in this chapter on page 107.

Dry Swings

The most overlooked and underrated practice of all is just taking cuts, no ball. When you're hitting a pitch, the swing happens so quickly that it's impossible to analyze exactly what's going on. With no ball, you focus more intensely on the pure mechanics of your swing. Dry swing everyday to groove and understand your swing. Work on specific areas: bat speed, leg drive, etc. Use the slow-motion and eyes closed gimmicks to help.

Training Tip: "Practice With a Heavier Bat"

Do all your training, including batting practice, with a slightly heavier bat than your "game one" to rocket performance.

You'll be shocked how much your bat speed increases without any special effort. This works fantastically. Use a bat only two to four ounces heavier, depending on player size and age.

The Sand Bat

This is for dry swinging only. For a super muscle strength trainer, get an old 27- or 28-inch bat. Drill out the knob and fill it with sand. Thread in an appropriate bolt to cap it. These bats will weigh about three to five pounds, so you'll want to choke up on the grip initially and work your way down as you get stronger. Grip down to make it as heavy as you can and still take quality swings. It makes great addition to the on-deck circle.

Medicine Ball Muscle

Mo Vaughn uses a heavy medicine ball to train explosive hip turn power and thrust.

Just hold the ball with both hands near the launch position and then heave it explosively; use your full hip turn and leg drive to propel it. It's best playing catch with a partner.

Use any old sports ball that's six or seven inches in diameter. Just pack in sand and stuffing through a slit and then duct tape the whole thing very securely.

The "Speed Stick" Bat Speed Trainer

This is for swinging only. You need strength and quickness training. Buy a piece of schedule 40 three-quarter-inch PVC pipe at any hardware store. Cut it off at your shoulder height. Now just make correct rips with it. It will tell you how fast you are swinging by the loudness of the whooshing sound it makes. The louder the faster. Have kids work in sets of seven or eight rips starting out medium and then speed up to maximum speed, little by little. This is particularly useful for kids who just seem to be dragging a slow bat — those who have no clue just how explosive and violent a swing should be. Speed sticks always seem to do a great job loosening up these kids and kicking them up into gears they never knew existed. A shorter length is great for Quick Twitch (see page 78). Speed sticks help diagnose problems as well, because they're very long and accentuate everything. They make it easier to see and feel aspects like uppercutting, sweeping, and hitching. It even works like a heavy bat because of high wind drag (see Figs. 10.2 and 10.3).

The Batting Tee

The batting tees can be used to learn and practice every aspect of a strong swing by yourself: grooving an accurate strike to the ball, hitting liners, developing hammer position power, and head work. It can guarantee a level swing. It is the ultimate reality check for your swing because you supply all the power. There is no varying energy supplied by the pitch itself. Always make your tee practice realistic by looking out at an imaginary pitcher and tracking an imaginary pitch to the tee (see Fig. 10.4).

Above: Fig. 10.2. Cut your speed stick to shoulder height.
Below: Fig. 10.3. Grip the speed stick and rip it. More noise means more speed.

Take it to an open field periodically to accurately gauge your current bat speed and power by distance. The humble batting tee can develop every foundation for a great swing.

Not bad for a twenty- or thirty-dollar investment.

Soft Toss

Soft toss is where a helper kneels safely to the side and underhands balls for you to hit, usually into some kind of backstop (see Fig. 20.5). Its big appeal is lots of quality repetitions with a moving ball in very little time. It's superb for head-to-the-bat, watch-it-disappear work. I think you'll find these passes a very important hurdle. Kids enjoy it enough that they actually want to do it, even without adult supervision. Tee and toss should be a staple of any batting practice. Soft toss is a big

Above: Fig. 10.4. Working with a tee, you can train most things by yourself.

Left: Fig. 10.5. Soft toss is great for practicing head to the bat, etc. and it's really fun to do.

104

time winner. It is very important that the tosser correctly feeds the balls out in front of the batter's hip. This allows the batter to practice making correct contact somewhere around the power positions.

Pepper

This drill has been around since the beginning of time because it works. You need at least one hitter and one thrower-fielder. The batter checks up, holds up, his swing at impact, trying to hit a ball back to the thrower. Do it right. Emphasize a crisp laser straight chop to the ball (see Fig. 10.6).

This drill is tremendous for headwork because

check-swinging makes it easier to see the ball to the bat. Make players "out" if they pull their heads. Few understand just how awesome pepper is. You are isolating and practicing the heart of the stroke — all the quick adjustments, manipulations, and contortions for driving the sweet spot to the ball. How huge is that? Great pepper players are always good hitters.

There are other hidden benefits: As players progress, the game becomes full of junk pitches because players try to eliminate each other. That's how pepper can often end up teaching lessons in off-speed pitch hitting and recognition.

Fig. 10.6. Pepper is very effective because you're practicing the heart of the swing.

The Sock Ball Drill

You take individual socks and roll them into balls which are then pitched to the guy hitting. To bat, the hitter just clasps his hands together and they are used to bat the thrown balls. This one is especially great with the youngest batters just starting out. That being said, it still works very well for any age, and is guaranteed fun. Pitchers can get pretty close to the batters for accuracy, because the socks are soft. Make sure you work on watching the contact and nose on the ball. This drill can be quickly done almost anywhere at any time. It's suitable for indoor use and needs little equipment or space. Using your hands to hit instead of a bat naturally trains your short, straight-to-the-ball swinging skills. This simplest of drills is unsurpassed for teaching how to pull your hands in on tight inside pitches (see "Starting Close" on page 34 and Fig. 5.5 on page. 54).

Wiffles

Hitting baseball-sized wiffles is the closest and most practical way to practice live arm hitting before games. It's not bad in practice either. Just be sure to try and throw directly down-wind. It works efficiently because the balls don't go all that far, allowing for lots of hits and quick pick-ups in a relatively short time and space.

Your Local Batting Cage

The benefits are obvious. Just follow these tips to get the most out of it. Methodically move around at the plate to work different locations and heights, especially weaknesses. Avoid hitting unrealistically fast speeds before games. If you must, make sure to hit realistic before you leave. Use cage speeds about 10 mph faster than what you expect in your next game. "Plus ten" is just about right. It seems to compensates for the fact that it's easier to pick up a machine ball release compared to one pitched by a live arm.

Coaching Tip: "Gift Wrapped"

Wrap your bat head with adhesive tape. The dirty cage balls will mark it with patterns that indicate your overall timing, early, late, or on time. It shows if you're hitting with the sweet spot. Clean it occasionally or re-tape.

Give Them a "Hand"

Hand strength makes a big difference. It's not only important for power, but also for bat control. Have youngsters squeeze your hand, and you'll see how little hand strength they have. Get players to carry around a tennis ball to squeeze. As they get stronger, you can add woodworking spring clamps of varying strength. The ultimate strength trainer, called a wrist roller, can be made from a plastic milk carton, some trimmer line, and a rod. This can be wound up and down with differing resistance according to how much water you use (see Figs. 10.7 and 10.8). Try some "wrist waggles." Hold any bat straight out in either hand.

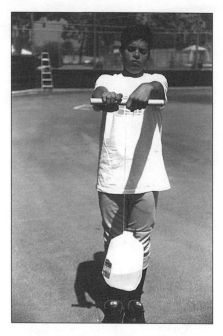

Above: Fig. 10.7. This simple device builds incredible hand and wrist strength.
Below: Fig. 10.8. Woodworking spring clamps or tennis balls are convenient

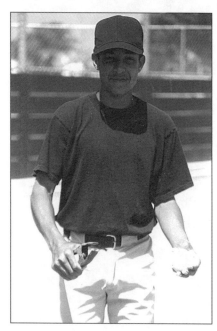

Now do slow "tomahawk chops" using only your wrist.

Sharp-Shooting Golf Wiffle Balls

Practice hitting golf ball size wiffles with a small diameter pipe cut to bat length. Use either schedule forty three-quarter inch PVC or one-half inch EMT with a handle built up with duct tape. Try to throw directly downwind, if there is any. Hitting these balls will automatically sharpen your focusing ability and increase your bat control a lot.

Full Contact Indoor Hitting — Without Guilt

We searched long and hard for the perfect ball to hit indoors, full power with a regular bat. The answer is ping pong balls.

You don't even need to move anything out of the way. I've never seen a ping pong ball break or even mark anything, even glassware. The small ball will definitely improve your aim and focus. In addition to regular throwing, try bouncing them off tables for fast accurate bounce pitches.

Home Practice Area

You can make an effective workout station with only a batting tee and a backstop. Backstops can be put up in a garage, backyard, or other suitable place by hanging an old piece of carpet or plastic shade cloth. Almost every aspect of hitting can be practiced without help off the tee. With a helper, you can add soft toss. It may not be the most exciting practice, but the results absolutely are.

11.

Advanced Hitting Skills

There are a few refinements you need to make in your seeing-the-ball skills at high levels. At advanced levels, many good pitchers will be very skilled at what is known as hiding the ball. What this means is they conceal their throwing arm and the ball from your view until the last instant by rotating it behind their back out of sight. If you don't use a special technique, the ball will often seem to literally "come out of nowhere" and you'll never get a "good look."

Advanced Hitting-the-Ball Stuff

Here's the method you can employ to pick up the release point of these crafty pitchers: The first thing you try to do is study and identify the basic location of the pitcher's release point. Relative to some part of his body, i.e. his head or shoulder. Then you want to imagine a small window at this location. Now, whenever a pitcher hides the ball, you can automatically shift you vision to your window to find the incoming pitch. With this technique, it will be very hard for any pitcher to hide the ball from you anymore.

Here is another subtle bit of knowledge that can benefit you as well: It is very hard for human beings to precisely hold an intense focus with their eyes for very long. What this ends up meaning for hitters is they should keep their gaze relatively relaxed, resting vaguely on the pitcher's face, until their arm goes back. Most people will simply not be able to maintain an intense focus if they start before this. If you have any doubts, just try to stare intensely for a while at a period on this page. If you're honest and perceptive with yourself, you will feel your focus "skip" a little very quickly. The key is to rest your eyes until you really need them. Only this way will you see the ball best during that critical fraction of a second between release and contact.

Hitting Offspeed

Ironically, the first key to hitting off-speed pitching is a solid swing that is effective hitting fastballs. Beyond that, the key

lies in being able to always step for a fastball, but keep your weight back and loaded for off-speed. This is done by separating properly. You always step for a fastball, because it's the only way you can hit one. You can slow your swing down, but not speed it up. That's what is meant by the wise saying, "Always look fastball, adjust for the curve."

Here's how you handle any offspeed pitch: The secret is proper separating as you stride. You must coil back as you step forward. Then whenever you see offspeed, you can just extend your backward coiling a little more, giving you that split second you need to adjust. This is what it means to "stay back"and "keep your hands back." It's separating that lets you swing immediately for a fastball or stay back totally loaded for offspeed.

Hitting Inside

Frequently on hard inside pitches, there isn't time to extend your arms and still get the bat head around in time. Good inside contact takes lots of skill.

The best hitters do this by abruptly pulling their hands in tight around in front of their body (see Figs. 11.1 and 11.2). This is often called "cranking the ball" because of the abrupt snapping turn, or "jerking the ball" because of the sharp inward pull. By abruptly shorten-

Figs. 11.1 (above) and 11.2 (below). Hitting inside pitching requires shortening up, pulling your hands rapidly around in front.

ing the arc of the swing this way, you drastically increase the inward course and speed of the bat head. For some lucky hitters, this "shortening up" just comes easy. For most it doesn't.

Instructing in this area is difficult. Hitting inside pitching is one area of hitting that can be described as more art than science. Good hitters compress and tighten up their swings only as much as necessary for each individual pitch. Everything changes radically according to how inside, high, or fast the pitch is.

Also, performance varies greatly depending on innate physical talents. Hitters have different reaction times. On the fast end, you have guys like Ken Griffey, Jr., who always seem to manage good extension at contact on everything inside or not, and rarely get jammed. Other mortal hitters, with slower reaction times, will often have to contort and cramp themselves into awkward looking impact positions, pulling their bat heads in on the ball.

Hence there isn't really any classic technique or perfect

form here. All that counts is results, period. Whenever you hit an inside pitch well, you know you're doing it right. Here are some things that can help you do that more often.

Improving Your Inside Hitting

1. You need to become good at performing the barrier drill. This trains you to properly stay close and compact early in your swing. A correct compact launch to begin with sets up the quickest possible tight inside rotation whenever you need it.

2. Go to a machine batting cage. There you can get slow, relatively consistent pitches. The method is to crowd the plate in varying degrees and work on your inside hitting techniques. Here's the big secret: Periodically check swing on some hits and freeze on contact, (like Pepper). Decide if you pulled your hands in effectively, and succeeded in making good contact on the sweet spot. If you did, study the position and commit that particular feel to memory as a job well done.

3. Another related and important way to practice is the check-swing game of Pepper. Just have the throwers give you lots of inside pitches. In Pepper, the batter tries to check-swing the ball back to the fielders that are mostly right in front of him, and not way out to the sides. To hit any inside toss back to the fielders, the batter must bring his hands way in, around in front of him like hitting inside pitches. Pepper will teach you how to pull the bat head in to make good contact. To foster even greater performance, you can easily make a special Pepper bat. Spray paint the sweet part of the barrel where ideal contact is desired with a bright stand-out color. Make it a rule that batters are "out" if they fail to hit the ball on the painted part.

4. Recently I stumbled upon the very best way to get the

feel and execution of "shortening up." It urns out that the unsung little "sock ball drill" is just huge (see page 54). This simplest of drills does a heck of a job teaching the hardest of skills. You'll remember, it conveyed the essence of the level chop swing. A few years ago, I was showing a kid the "sock ball drill," and fortunately I threw way inside a couple of times by mistake. Oh, well, it only took me five years to realize what had been right in front of my face. Better late, than never. Do the "sock ball drill. Tell your pitcher to mix things up, but definitely throw inside regularly. In no time, you'll experience exactly what it means and how it feels to "shorten up."

"Don't Tense Up, Stay Loose."

You hear this so much in athletics, you can't help but know it's true. This one is used so much it's a cliche. The problem with cliches is we tend not to examine them. In this case, that would be disastrous.

You need to know what physical tension really means and understand why it's desirable to be loose in the first place. Only then can you really achieve it. Many of the important muscles in the body work in opposing pairs. In your upper arm, for example, the triceps and biceps work as an opposing pair to either straighten out your arm or bend it back.

If your arm is all tensed up, you are somewhat contracting both opposing muscles at the same time. To straighten your arm, you will be fighting against yourself. This is how tension slows movement. Staying loose without tensing lets you powerfully contract the specific muscles you want with minimum resistance from opposing and supporting ones.

Getting a Good Pitch to Hit

It's no coincidence that the last hitter to hit over four hundred was Ted Williams. He was fanatic about finding a good pitch to hit. He drew a lot of walks, not just because of his dangerous power, but because he had discipline. The best hitters are extremely smart and controlled. They consistently work the count, making it much more likely to get a good pitch that they can drive. Here's how—you will almost always want to do the following up until you have two strikes:

1. Obviously, take any ball.

2. Take any pitch, even strikes, that you can't drive or likely hit hard. This is the big secret: You don't want to hit a pitcher's pitch for an easy out. There are two main mistakes. Trying to hit, or even pull, a low pitch that's off the outside edge of the plate. It's hard to hit, especially with power. If you try to pull it like so many do, it's likely a weak ground ball out to the shortstop. The second mistake is swinging at high pitches well up in the zone. "Up in your eyes," as they say. Smart hitters learn to lay off any pitches above their hands. As good as these of-

ten look, they're very hard to catch up with or get on top of, because of gravity. They result in lots of undercut whiffs or pop-ups. When a good pitcher sees you'll swing at his pitch, it's always trouble. He'll just work that area, a little bit more and more out of the zone.

Becoming a Smart Hitter

Study how the pitcher is working. How wild or accurate is he? How fast? Does he seem to always throw a first-pitch, fastball strike? What is his out-pitch and where does he like to throw it? Is he throwing his breaking stuff for strikes? Is he tipping those when he in the glove? What is his two-strike waste pitch? This is a pitch well out of the zone he hopes you will go fishing for. Does he favor certain areas of the zone? Last, but not even close to least, what is the zone the umpire is calling? Based on your observations, you can come to the plate with a plan to hit. This is based on knowing your strengths and how the pitcher's throwing. Smart hitters make adjustments to situations.

1. It's often a good idea to crowd the plate a little so you can cover pitches off the plate outside a couple of inches (excepting real hard throwers). In youth leagues, all but the fastest pitchers will try to work the outside corner. Sad to say, this is also because umpires often tend to call strikes a couple of inches off the plate here.

2. For pitchers who like to get you with or other low pitching, you want to move up in the box and "take that away." Unfortunately, many umpires also regularly tend to call low pitches strikes out of the zone too. By moving up in the box, the pitcher has to "bring the ball up" for you if he wants to throw a called strike, even with bad umpiring.

3. With no-strikes always, look for a very good pitch to hit, appropriately called a belt-buckle strike. Unless the pitcher is very dominating, take the mind-set of looking for a good pitch up to two strikes. The more the count becomes in your favor, the more particular you want to be. With a three and zero, or three and one count, you want to do what is known as "zoning the ball": You look for a great pitch right in a little tight window that you can really drive hard. Only swing if you see that "sweet" pitch right there in your window.

4. If a pitcher's really wild or struggling, wait for him to throw you a strike before you even think of swinging. If you're well behind late in a game, and desperately need lots of base runners, you might want to adopt this "take a strike" strategy.

5. If you face any real hard thrower who's not wild, make up your mind to try and get out in front of his first fast ball to get your timing geared up quickly.

If he's really a "flame thrower," throwing strikes, think of trying to hit the ball pretty much "right out of his hand." Try to be aggressive right from the start. Come out strong from the "get go." Don't be afraid to step early to try to time-out heat. Fact is, you almost never see batters missing because they're too early on really fast pitching. Sometimes, just getting around, fouling off or even missing on time, with a guy who considers himself fast can really upset pitchers.

Two-Strike Hitting

With two strikes:

1. Choke up an inch on your bat for more quickness.

2. Plan and step to hit every pitch right up until you don't.

3. Step for a fastball, adjust for the curve.

4. Take away the most threatening location. Usually this will be outside and low. The exception is a pitcher throwing real heat.

5. Here's the biggie: It's for any situation where you desperately want at least a single, either for yourself or the team, like knocking in the tying or go-ahead run. Concentrate on hitting a hard "top half" grounder up the middle right through the pitcher. Some guys like to think of this as trying to "knock the knee caps off the pitcher." Up the middle provides the most expansive hole, and trying to hit a ground ball minimizes missing under the ball. The overwhelming type of whiff.

Coaching Tip: "Back Through the Middle"

Good coaches will have hitters actually work on this regularly in batting practice: Use a pitching screen and give points for hitting it with solid hits.

The bottom line goal for two-strike hitting is to put the ball in play. Your job is to battle. This means fighting off great pitches, fouling them off. If you're really desperate, try shortening up your swing and punch the ball like Pepper, but a little sharper and harder. I know hitters who "make a living," as they say, "punching" the ball just over the infield. You'll be amazed how far you can hit a power-position check-swing.

6. If the umpire is calling pitches that are four inches outside as strikes, you better swing at them. Even if you know the pitch really was a rule-book ball, it doesn't feel any less horrible walking back to the dugout getting called out. It definitely is better to go down swinging when you have an umpire who has, shall we say, questionable eyesight.

7. If in doubt, swing. The timeless cliché "anything close" is great advice.

Advanced Hitting Aspiring to Greatness — the Razor's Edge

Everything about being great instead of good comes down to hundredths of a second. Mark Maguire's swing is a scant five hundredths of second quicker than the average major leaguer. Yet this difference is the razor's edge to hall of fame performance. Take a lesson. If you have an insatiable desire for greatness here's what you'll need:

1. Tremendous hand and wrist strength. Tireless wrist roller work. Strong quick hands are devastating weapons for hitting.

2. Heavy sand bat training and speed stick work. Do dry swing training in speed cycles starting from medium and gradually building to maximum. Really push your top end, relentlessly trying to cut every single thousandth off swing time. Always do all your batting practice with a training bat two to four ounces heavier than your game bat.

3. Relentless dry swinging and clasp hands only work on an ever more explosive body turn and hip pivot. This is incredibly impor-

tant. Furious and determined power batting tee work everyday, minimum 100 balls. Try to literally crush every ball in a dead line drive. If you can get someone to soft-toss you a hundred more, even better. You can only perfect bat head speed by working on it hard. Never accept any limits. Try to make your air blast louder and louder. Make bat speed and quickness an ego trip you're immeasurably proud of. This is the head trip that will help motivate you to never settle.

4. Most importantly, adopt an unbelievably enthusiastic attitude about performing all the unglamourous work described above.

Secrets for "Raising the Bar"

In your quest for greatness, you're bound to hit periods where you're certain there's just no way to further improve your performance. Realize this is natural — but also a complete load of bull. Greatness is limitless. You just need to know how to raise the bar.

Now you're totally convinced your swing can't get any quicker. You've worked your butt off as it is. You're absolutely sure there's no way, nohow, for you to get one spec quicker. Want to bet on it? Dry swing your bat until you believe you're flat out maxed. Next, pick up a heavy sand bat or add a heavy doughnut to yours. Now, swing this super weight fiercely, truly bent on equaling or even surpassing the previous speed level attained with your normal bat.

Then swing your regular bat one final time. Genuinely challenge your speed limits once again. You're sure to novice the startling fact that you were quite mistaken about having already reached your ultimate potential. Accept that the human body is capable of almost anything. Almost always more than the mind thinks is possible. It just needs the right kind of push.

You only thought you had reached your full potential. The question is, what do you do to get your body to consistently perform at that higher level without having to fool it with the weighted bat trick? After all, your body has obviously proved itself capable of more than you ever thought possible.

The bar has been raised. But, how do you jump it?

The secret is to now focus more narrowly on all the individual segments of your swing, To "jump the bar," you will want to work in turn on increasing the performance of each separate area. This might include individual alternating attention on increasing the quickness of your: hands, wrists, hips, rear foot pivot, or shoulders for example.

Here's the lesson: Accept, there's always more greatness to explore. It's just in the details more.

12.

Winning the Mental Game

The key is to realize that you can control your thinking by regularly practicing specific thoughts and feelings. It shouldn't be any different than practicing your stride for example.

Sole Swing Thought

In games, at the moment the ball is pitched, you want to be concentrating entirely on only one thing: "seeing the ball." You want to train really hard in practice so that everything else in games is reflex.

Seeing the ball is the only act that helps you contact that one pitch, at that one moment. Equally important, it keeps you from thinking about anything else — specifically, any kind of worrying thought about strik-ing out or swinging level, etc. (See page 48, "Lightning in a Bottle" for the only other re-lated swing thought you should consider). Any negative thought, or even apparently good ones about proper tech-nique, are not productive. They just distract from the crucial act of the moment — "seeing the ball."

You need to practice this, like anything else. Part of the time in batting practice, work on clearing your mind except for "seeing the ball." Now practice it, creating imaginary pressure situations, like bases loaded, or two strikes.

Everyone agrees that confidence is crucial to hit well. This is your secret weapon against being nervous or doubtful. The more pressure-packed the situation, the more it helps. It's a scientific fact that human beings can't think of two things at once. If you're fully concentrating on "seeing the ball," it prevents you from feeling or thinking about pressure, or anything else for that matter. You can learn that the more pressure, the more intensely you concentrate on "seeing the ball." Developing this "tunnel vision" gives you a huge advantage.

Coaching Tip: "Thinking Ahead"

This doesn't mean you shouldn't be thinking about proper technique before the pitcher winds up. On the contrary, you should be doing a pre-swing routine and visualizing and anticipating success (see page 72,"Hammer Rehearsal").

You can learn to plug these positives into your subconscious. Then when the pitcher delivers, "see the ball" will work even better.

Coaching Tip: "Tough Love, the Two Strike Drill"

Make hitting under pressure part of batting practice. Use the "two-strike drill." Players line up and start with two strikes. Any miss puts them out. Have a maximum pitch number or the best hitters will eat up all the time or, worse, hitters will just start taking defensive contact swings. Create many imaginary pressure-packed scenarios.

Positive Thinking in the On-Deck Circle/ Visualization

Your proper mental and physical preparation in the on-deck circle is crucial for your best hitting. While on deck, you should always "time-out" the pitcher. That means you practice timing strong rips at any pitches he delivers to the plate from afar. Rehearse the right mental images each time as well. Intensely visualize yourself hammering each pitch in a line shot every swing. You are setting yourself up to be successful with this positive thinking. This is rehearsing to be confident and focused.

It is undisputed fact that these positive mental exercises will help improve your performance. How stupid would you be to blow this off.

Coping with Failure

Hitting is full of failure. Even in little league, the best fail about half the time. To cope, you need to do one very special thing. Become your own number one fan. You do this by celebrating successes, finding satisfaction in positives, big and small, and taking genuine pride in effort for its own sake.

Overdo it. Fan stands for fanatic. Appreciate every little thing. Anytime you get a good rip at the ball, practice feeling satisfied. Not delighted or overjoyed, but satisfied, no matter what. Particularly important is to feel very good about any

hard-hit ball, regardless if it's an out or hit. Practice really congratulating yourself on your defense, walks, moving the runner, sacrificing, taking out the second baseman, fake bunts, slides, picking up signs, and so on.

After any failure, practice drowning out the bad taste with memories of previous hits, plays, or other positives.

Get really involved in rooting for your team mates. Learn to enjoy their successes like your own. Tell yourself what a great team player you are, or how hard you try.

In fact, that is the big key. There's one thing you really want to take to heart, the sooner the better. If you tried really hard to give your best effort, then feel very good and proud of that. Not being afraid to fail and giving your all is what helps you to be successful your next at bat and for the rest to come. Go way out of your way to celebrate the positives, big and little, and drown out the negative That's what your number-one fan would do.

Fearful Batters

If there's one thing a youth batting instructor is familiar with, it's fearful batters. It goes with the territory. Here's what helps:

You've got to start by facing some facts. Getting hit is part of the game. At some point, you'll just have to get over your fear or quit. The real possibility of getting hit won't go away. Fearful batters often end up wanting pity and having people feel sorry for them. Face it, that attitude just doesn't help or change anything. How about something that actually will help?

Time for your whole new attitude in batting practice. Really, how much worse can it get? Start over. Time for something different, for a change. Make this your attitude: "I'm just going to kill the ball, that's it. I'm sick and tired of this crud and I'll show that stupid "blankety-blank ball." Get mad at the ball for a change, not scared. It can't be any worse than that knotted stomach, scared, sick feeling, right? You won't be as scared when you're mad. You're fed up. Time to bash it to pieces. Try swinging furiously at the ball. Try getting really mad. Get even.

How Parents Can Help

Assuming you're in youth baseball, talk to your parents about paying you just for bravery. Maybe twenty five to fifty cents a pitch. Have your parents read the material that follows. It's a good idea for you to read it too.

Parents: set up monetary reward in baby steps, depending on how scared you think your child is. Like just for standing in the box strong to begin with. Like for not doing the two-step characteristic of really scared batters, stepping out with the back foot first, closely followed by the front. Then maybe paying for standing tough and taking any strong cut, no matter what the result. Then pay for any contact, etc.

With patience and thoughtful analysis about what you want to reward and encourage, you can get results. Make sure to absolutely lavish huge amounts of verbal praise as well about how incredible proud you are of their bravery. Remember to talk about and reward bravery, not the results. Don't be hesitant to let players backslide as necessary. Just resume patiently racketing up the goals again as soon as possible. With lots of patience and encouragement — and a little money — this works.

Desensitization

Employ the additional strategy concurrently as well: Routinely go to a machine batting cage. Initially, have the scared batter enter and then stand well back from the plate in a cage throwing at very high speed. Twenty or thirty mph greater than his own level if possible. Patiently let him just stand there. It may take a while, but eventually he will calm down. I've seen scared batters even flinch at first. Once he accepts that the balls, although scarily fast, actually won't hit him, he can take the next step, literally.

Have him slowly edge his way forward until he's in a proper stance reasonably close to the plate. Now urge him to take some swings. He will naturally be pathetically late, but that's not even the point. If he's

totally reluctant, don't force it. The main thing is that he just stand in there until he's completely calm. It can take a while, so be patient. At this point, have the player go into a cage throwing at his appropriate speed level, and really try to hit there. With any luck, his customary fear level for this normal pitching will have diminished a whole lot. Stick with it. Try repeating the whole sequence for a while. It's based on a proven psychological technique called "desensitization" and I've seen it work wonders.

Setting Goals and Incentives

Parents and coaches can use incentives to discourage or encourage any behavior they select — in games or practice. They should always be realistic but challenging. If the reward is money, the amount must be sensible. You want to avoid the terrible mistake of paying too much money. Often this will backfire by putting too much pressure on the kids. They should meet common-sense guidelines. Kids should never feel devastated because they didn't get the money. It must be something the batter is glad to get but no big deal if he doesn't. Any parent should know his own kids well enough to make sensible decisions here.

Coaching Tip for Coaches: "Pain and Gain"

The customary form of disincentive used by coaches is extra running. Instead, try more productive techniques, like push-ups and or sit-ups. Running takes more time, often reducing and disrupting practice. Calisthenics also do more to improve hitting specifically.

It pays to plan very carefully exactly what you are trying to get. For example, my system for my own kids in games pays $1.50 for singles, $4 for doubles, $6 for triples, and $8 for a home run. Because my kids almost always make contact, this plan is specifically designed to get them to try to hit for power and be very aggressive. Hence the considerable gap between singles and doubles. There is only a penalty for striking out looking, never for swinging. Notice that the home run bounty is not overly inflated. If you've been paying attention, you know that wanting to swing for the fences is never a good idea.

When you design your plan, sit down and give it a lot of thought about what you want. Be creative. There are lots of things you might want to reward for games or practice. Any hard-hit ball, aggressive swings, line drives. There are probably things you may want to discourage by reducing reward with specified penalties. Like stepping in the bucket, swinging at high pitches, pulling the head, etc. Remember, you can always change or modify them as necessary. If you have a set practice routine scheduled for your kid, it's not a bad idea to pay a small weekly allowance for this work. Used responsibly with lots of common sense, goals and incentives — including money — can be powerful tools to improve hitting performance.

13.

Troubleshooting

I'm even more expert in bad hitting than good. Let's face it, most people don't come to a batting instructor because they're tearing the cover off the ball. There's a positive. My immense experience with bad hitting makes this section all the more powerful. Over the years, you recognize what trouble really is and exactly what to do about it.

Almost every problem you have will fall into one of three categories. Poor performance will almost always be associated with one or more of these three: pulling the head, uppercutting, or being late. Not surprisingly, these are the exact opposites of the three keys to hitting: head to the bat, level swing, and out in front contact.

Pulling the Head and Not Seeing the Ball

This problem is ironically the most underestimated. Until this book came out, no one had bothered to offer any real solutions or corrective drills. Watching the ball all the way to the bat seems simple but is just the opposite. Unlike other aspects of hitting, you never master it. You have to work on the habit constantly to maintain it, for as long as you play baseball.

Symptoms: Missing, strike outs.

How to spot it: Just watch the nose. If the nose doesn't turn downward toward the contact point the batter is not seeing the ball all the way to the bat.

Correction: First, understanding the challenge. Then nose catch, bat catch, net catch, and the seven step-by-step head-to-the-bat practice techniques. Everything about good hitting starts with seeing the ball to the bat.

Uppercutting

Batters miss by swinging under non offspeed pitches ninety percent of the time. Upper-cutting just makes this natural tendency even worse. You will never hit to your potential with an uppercut. Because the bat head drops well below the plane of the incoming pitch, it demands perfect timing to get consistent solid contact.

Symptoms: Inconsistency, missing and strike-outs, particularly on high heat, long high-fly ball outs, pop-ups, and ironically lots of topped weak ground balls.

Fig. 13.1. Rear foot block locks out the hip turn.

Fig. 13.2. A proper foot pivot like this is vital for complete rotation.

How to spot it: The arc of the hands and the bat head will look like a happy face smile, short and curvy on both ends. The bat will consistently be headed uphill at the ball. Proper level swings look much straighter, downward, and longer, like a swish shape. Uppercutting can often result from hitching. If a batter hitches his hands down, it can force him to swing uphill at high pitches in the strike zone.

Correction: Understanding and accepting it as a big problem with its inevitable negative results. The two-tee drill, the swish drill.

Swinging Late — Rear Foot Block

If your rear foot does not pivot and rotate up, like mashing a bug, you can't effectively rotate the hips or body (see Figs. 13.1 and 13.2). This blocks out power and speed.

Symptoms: Players who seems to always swing late and can't handle inside. This is the most common problem you see in young batters.

What to look for: Just watch the rear foot to see if it rotates up properly (see Fig. 13.2) or stays locked on the ground or hardly turns.

Symptoms: always being late, slow, weak swings that seem to stop short.

Correction: Three spots drill (see page 88 for hitching)

"Dead Hands"

The hands must cock backward before they go forward. This cocking action overcomes inertia making your bat quicker.

The Little Kids' Swing Syndrome — Weight Shift Slide Style Hitting

Most little kids instinctively swing trying to slide the weight and power to the ball, without sufficient turning of the hips (see Fig. 13.3). Often this swing is started with dead hands and an overly long stride over strid-

Above: Fig. 13.3. Weight slide hitting with weak turning of the hips is inefficient.
Below: Fig. 13.4. To hit best, you need a short stride and a full turn.

ing. The upper body is left to supply most of the power. This can work adequately at lower levels, but in the long run it gets you nowhere. When ball speeds climb above forty, this primitive swing doesn't hold up, particularly on inside pitches.

Symptoms: The batter is constantly late, especially on inside pitches. They will often seem to "give up and bail out," not wanting to get another "stinger" from not being able to get the bat head around on inside pitches. Watch the back foot pivot carefully to see if it actually turns, and carefully evaluate how much the belt buckle actually turns to face the pitcher on a middle in pitch. Rotation is often as little as thirty percent of a proper full turn. To hit well, you need a short stride and a full turn, rotational hitting, never a long slide and a slight turn (see Fig. 13.4).

Correction: Refer to sections on the three spots drill as well as "dead hands." For overstriding, the section on "No Stride" will be helpful.

129

Very commonly, hitters without any great flaws still tend toward swinging late anyway. This is because the natural instinct is to hit the ball right in front of the middle of your body. If you don't see any obvious flaw, the solution lies in replacing your natural late habits by working hard on the out-in-front and hammer rehearsal drills.

14.

Conclusions

You need to get the "big picture." Then you can concentrate hardest on what counts the most. In batting, there are three special skills that really matter.

How well you hit depends mainly on how well you do the master keys to hitting: watching the ball to the bat, "out in front" contact, and level swinging (no uphill swinging). Understand that these are skills that must be learned. They never come naturally or easily to human being, that's why there are so many weak hitters. They demand lots of practice and hard work. It will be worth it. I have never seen any batter who did these three well and who was not an extremely good hitter.

Below is an outline plan for learning the keys. Each of the master skills has a few key drills that most effectively teach its essentials. While there are many other lesser drills, make sure to tackle these main ones first. They are the core. If you do these drills enough, you are guaranteed too book results. I have never seen otherwise.

I want to warn you: You have just been handed the true keys to hitting. Now it's all up to you to "step up to the plate and go deep." Knowing what they are is easy. Spending hours practicing them is another thing.

The painful truth is that many hitters will fail only because they lack the discipline to do the necessary hard, and sometimes boring, work. If you ever want to be a great hitter, you cannot let that be you.

Master Skills and Drills Outline

Important: this assumes that you have already mastered the proper set-up exactly before beginning these. See that you do the following:

1. Head on the ball all the way to the bat:

   ❏ Nose and bat catch (see page 43)

   ❏ "Head to the bat" routine. All six steps (see page 43)

   ❏ Twang (see page 51)

2. No uphill swings / level swing:

   ❏ "Tee and stick" drill (see page 69)

3. Out in front contact:

   ❏ The "barrier" drill (see page 87)

   ❏ The "spotlight" drill (see page 82)

   ❏ The "out in front"drill (see page 72)

   ❏ The "hammer" drill (see page 73)

A Step-by-Step Fail-Proof Plan

I defy anyone to conscientiously work at this system and not become a good hitter. Do it with commitment and passion and you will succeed.

1. Master the set up (see pages 21–37)

2. Practice and learn the chop swing (see page 53):

   ❏ Hand and sock drills (see page 53)

   ❏ Twang (see page 51)

3. Practice and understand head-to-the-bat (see page 43):

   ❏ Nose and bat catch (see page 43)

❏ The seven batting practice steps and three drill (see pages 44–49)

4. Practice the tee-and-stick drill to eliminate uppercutting (see page 69):

   ❏ Line drive tee work (see page 66)

5. Practice the hammer and out-in-front drills (see pages 77 and 62):

   ❏ The spotlight and barrier drills (see pages 81 and 84)

   ❏ Tennis racket trainer (see page 77)

15.

Teaching Wizardry for Coaches—Keeping Their Attention

Here's a "three-pronged" attack that keeps kids engaged and actively participating every step. First, dust off the oldest trick in the book. Ask questions to teach: This makes kids pay close attention because they have to think and talk. Ask lots of questions like what do you know about a level swing? Why do you think swinging level is important?

Once you see the amazing results, you'll get in the habit. An added side benefit is that you'll constantly know whether you're getting through and be able to catch any misunderstandings immediately.

Right along with your questions, use this trick: Ask the kids to show you they know what you mean. Have them physically demonstrate what they think you're getting at every opportunity. Even with these tricks, some kids will tune you out. Learn to spot drifting eyes. That's your cue to break out your third weapon: forcefully point two fingers at your eyes and demand: "Eyes here!" and wait for absolute compliance. Together, these three tricks can't fail to command the attention you need to teach.

Coaching Tip: "What Did I Just Say?"

Whenever you suspect you don't have their attention, try this: Just ask them in a very stern tone, "What did I just say?" It's shocking how often they won't know; but at least, then you can do something about it.

Teaching Tips: The Terrific Ten

These are the methods and techniques that have been touched on throughout this text. They represent a very powerful arsenal for getting results.

1. Slow-motion and frame-by-frame;

2. Eyes closed;

3. Hands-only drills, swings, hands clasped;

4. Forward and then backward tracing, retracing numerous times;

5. Exaggeration and over-correction, stop as soon as possible;

6. Reducing the swing to parts, or even parts of parts;

7. Practicing constructive mental thoughts and feelings

8. Using your ears for sound;

9. Using your imagination/ visualization, e.g. "cut it in half," imaginary barrier drill, etc.;

10. Doing corrective training drills between pitches in batting practice.

Coaches Appendix 1

Vital Coaching Phrases: "Say the Magic Words"

Here are some powerful phrases I use for the key areas so much that I hear them in my sleep. They are indeed "magic." I will identify what area they cover, and whether they are for practice only, game time only, or both.

Seeing the Ball:

❏ "See the ball, cut it exactly in half!"game time or practice.

❏ "Keep your nose on the ball" or "stick your nose on the hit!" practice and game time.

❏ "Watch the ball hit your bat, watch it disappear, don't see where it goes, stare at the ground!" practice only.

❏ "Watch the ball the last three feet!" practice only.

Swinging Level:

❏ "No uphill swings!" game or practice.

❏ "Chop your hands straight to the ball!"game or .practice.

❏ "Fire your hands in a straight line to the ball!" game time or practice.

❏ "Swing downhill through the ball," practice only for uppercutters.

Out in Front Timing:

❏ "Hit the ball out in front of your eyes — where you can see it best!" game time or practice; use this constantly in games.

❏ "Don't be afraid to swing too early!" practice only.

❏ "Hit it right out of his hand!" game time only, for use only against exceptionally fast dominating pitching.

Coaching Tip: "Never Say Don't"

You'll notice that all these phrases have something very important in common: They all ask for a positive affirmative action. They instruct the batters to do something positive, not "don't do this or that." Telling players not to do something doesn't work well in games. It's way too complicated to process, and it actually puts negatives in the batter's mind. If you feel you absolutely must use a don't, always follow it with one of the affirmative phrases.

Coaches Appendix 2

Conducting a Quality Batting Practice

Assuming you have absorbed the essentials of this book, you and at least one other coach should now be able to put together the world's finest batting and swing practice. You'll notice the "and swing" part, I'm sure. This is because, through ignorance or otherwise, many coaches are content to just worry about getting their players to hit as well as they can with whatever swing they have, no matter how flawed. This is far less work, but if you love and respect the game, let alone your players, you'll never even consider it.

Fortunately, the world's finest swing part of your practice can largely be entrusted to some great solitary training tools in this book. These are: the "twang," the "speed stick," the "barrier drill," the "uppercut breaker tee," the "spotlight drills," and the "tire." What makes these so great from a coaching standpoint is that they can be practiced by the batter on his own and still work without supervision. This is an incredible luxury. As any coach will tell you, the main problem in practices is guys standing around doing nothing, waiting in line to do something. With these tools, you should be able to get lots of value out of every minute of batting practice.

You can count on a few more training methods requiring only two players to complete the quality swing development you're after. These are: nose and bat catch, net catch, tee and soft toss, and wiffles. Here's how you can construct an ideal batting practice by integrating all these tools into it. Your batting practice will constantly train and emphasize the three principles of the "WIN" system. Watch the ball to the bat, in front contact, and no up hill swings — swing level.

At some point, your routine batting practice will involve three stations and run like clockwork. The secret to making sure this happens is to start your season in the form of a group clinic. The ultimate performance of all your hitters will depend on achieving the following goals before you go on:

1. A solid squared-up stance and set-up for every player.

2. Thorough understanding of the coil, separate, and launch swing mechanics.

3. Total group understanding of the use and purpose of all the tools at all the stations.

4. Total group understanding and commitment to hitting line drives and hard grounders.

Once these objectives are met, your team will be ready for the routine three station batting practice.

For a twelve-man team, there will be four players at each station for approximately forty minutes.

Then they will rotate to the next station.

Station One: Swing Building

This station will employ the following drills and tools to train and build the swing quality of all your players. Because there are eight components, each player will rotate every five minutes or so.

Note:

Go out and buy some egg timers for this purpose. Nothing else will do. I know this from experience. A watch never works. There's just too much going on, and prompt rotation is totally critical. If you don't have a coach at station one, put a reliable kid leader in charge of resetting the clock. Here are the eight aspects:

Activity/Advice

1. The "twang:" It's critical to imagine a pitch and track it to the painted tip of the hose. Try imagining different speeds

2. The "barrier drill:" Put a target, belt-high on fence.

3. "Uppercut breaker tee:" Use wiffles if you have to keep all the activities in close proximity.

4. "High speed spot light drill:" Do hands only version to increase focus on the mechanic.

5. The "speed stick:" Do sets of swings from medium to maximum velocity, then three more at top speed.

6. The "tire:" The key is to get max "pop" right at impact.

7. The "sand bat:" Choke it up as far as you have to swing it correctly.

8. "Wrist rollers:" Wind it both up and down.

All station-one activities are solitary. This I can guarantee: If a coach is not there to push them, the kids will always start goofing off and just go through the motions. Like most hitting work, this stuff isn't glamorous or very exciting. You will most certainly want to crack the whip early on and make it absolutely clear that you won't tolerate crappy effort. I really urge you to jump on them the first time you see slackers with this admonition: "Anybody doesn't take this dead serious and everybody runs!"

Back it up. If you don't have a coach, try recruiting a parent to make them work hard.

Station Two: Players Plus Coach Tee, Toss, and Darts

Four players in total. Three players on wiffles, one player with coach, and one player rotates every ten minutes.

A coach works one player each rotation on tee and soft toss, then throws wiffle darts from close range with screen or face guard. The wiffle-dart format will be the same as outlined below for the players.

Concurrently, three other players are hitting wiffles in rotation, with one thrower, one shagger, and a hitter. Rotation the same, every ten minutes.

There will be a rigidly set wiffle routine. It requires in order: five bunts, five net-catch check-swings, five ground balls, at least ten perfectly executed watch-it-disappear cuts, five two-strike attempts, and minimum ten see-it, crush-it swings.

Important note:

If the batter hits under, up foul, or pop up two balls in a row anytime during this last phase, he is automatically out and loses his turn.

When space is a problem, try putting the coach and kid wiffle thrower back to back. They can protect each other's backs, and the groups can keep swapping balls which will naturally be closer one way or the other. You can screen the coach or have him wear head guards if desired. Having a coach literally right in the middle of the players is extremely desirable from a supervision standpoint.

Station Three: Live-Arm (Preferably) or Machine Batting Practice

Four guys, forty minutes, ten minutes each rotation. Same set routine but with regulation distance and real balls. To use the net catch check swing part, you'll have to construct a very strong net. It may

also be helpful to use a pitching machine, if available, for the bunting and check swinging to keep the live arms fresher and extend them.

Important:

Add the No. 3 drill to the watch-it-disappear phase. Also add the out-in-front drill and hammer rehearsal practice if there is time. Ten minutes often seems a lot longer than you think.

Creating and Maintaining Focus

Don't let the inmates run the jail. If you leave it to the players, this is what I guarantee will occur: They'll just gradually, and slyly, end up trying to see how far they can all hit with nice juicy uppercuts. The worst thing possible.

Inform your players in no uncertain terms that batting practice is now and for all time line-drive practice, no ifs, ands, or buts — even for your biggest power hitters. Clearly communicate exactly how that goal is to be practiced and ultimately met. At a minimum, make these concepts the "law" for your team.

Have brief team meetings regularly to generate focus. Reiterate the necessity of hitting line drives and hard grounders. Review the importance of never trying to lift the ball. See that they "get" and buy into the concept, that missing almost always results from being late or swinging under. Revisit the discipline of top-half/get-on-top for two-strike hitting. Institute the practice of having batters doing push-ups and or sit-ups after their batting practice session based on the number of hit balls that were not driven.

Here are five coaching phrases you want to "wear out" in batting practice — and, actually, in games as well:

1. "Keep your nose on the ball!"

2. "Cut the ball exactly in half!"

3. "Line drives and hard grounders!"

4. "Hit the ball out in front, where you can see it best!"

5. "Stay level, swing straight to the ball!"

What a coincidence: These phrases all pertain to the three master principles of hitting. Watching the ball to the bat, in-front contact, and no uphill swings.

Coaching Tip: "Me and My Shadow"

Inform your team that it is not acceptable to just stand around. Institute the policy of "mirroring." If a batter ever finds himself just watching somebody else working, usually waiting his turn at a drill or exercise, instruct them that they are now expected to mirror and match that busy individual swing for swing.

Bibliography

Carew, Rod with Frank Pace and Armen Keteyian. *Rod Carew's Art and Science of Hitting*. New York: Viking Penguin Inc., 1986.

Lau, Charley with Alfred Glossbrenner. *The Art of Hitting 300*. Revised and Updated by Tony Larusssa. New York: Penguin Books, 1984.

Gwynn, Tony with Jim Rosenthal. *Tony Gwynn's Total Baseball Player*. New York: St. Martin's Press, 1992.

Baker, Dusty, Jeff Mercer and Marv Bittinger. *You Can Teach Hitting*. Indianapolis, IN: Masters Press, 1993.

Schmidt, Mike and Rob Ellis. *The Mike Schmidt Study*. Atlanta, GA: McGriff and Bell, Inc., 1994.

Williams, Ted with John Underwood. *The Science of Hitting*. New York: Simon and Schuster, 1971.

Rose, Pete and Peter Golenbock. *Pete Rose on Hitting: How to Hit Better than Anybody*. Berkley Publishing Group, 1985.

Boggs, Wade and David Brisson. *The Modern Science of Hitting*. Putnam Publishing Group, 1960.

Delmonico, Rod. *Hit and Run Baseball*. Leisure Press, 1992.

Alston, Walter Emmons. *The Complete Baseball Handbook*. Boston: Allyn and Bacon., 1972.

Kreuter, Peter, and Ted Kerley. *Little League's Official How-To-Play Baseball Book*. New York: Doubleday, 1990.

Orange County Register, Tuesday September 8, 1998, "Baseball," sports section, p. 6.

Index